INSIDE OUT

Tales of an Undercover Detective
by Dale Snipes as told by Jerry

While most of this book is based on actual events, names have been changed to protect the innocent. Events have been somewhat modified and journalistic pleasures taken. Therefore, no names or events can be taken as fact. This is a work of fiction and should not be linked to anyone.

Available from Amazon.com
Kindle and other retail outlets

The gang put a hit on him. Not for doing his job
but for violating the brotherhood!
He left the court house and was heading up James
Street. Cars were honking at a car going the wrong
way and heading for him. He saw the gang's old Plymouth and a shot gun poking out the window, aimed at
him! He jumped the curb, drove up the sidewalk
and up the freeway on ramp just as his rear window
was shot out. Jerry drove clear to Olympia before he
stopped and called in to report it.

Dedication

To Jerry J. for allowing me to pick
his brain for all the long hours over
the last year. To Gary Lee, for his invaluable
help in getting the book ready to print and
for all the friends and family who helped
with the proof reading throughout the
year it took to get it all together.

INSIDE OUT

Chapter 1
What Started it All

Detective Jerry Jorgenson had been working under-cover cases for some time, one morning a call came in to the station from a big name band that was in town for a concert. They had been staying in one of the area's finest hotels and had their semi-truck out front with all their equipment and instruments in it. The whole semi was stolen. Just about 15 minutes before that Jerry's dept. got a call from an informant that said he had heard about some men that had a whole lot of music equipment for sale and were looking for a "fence". The incident had not been in the news, so they talked to the informant and got the rest of the details about the men selling the equipment.

Jerry and his partner Ted, made arrangements to meet the high jackers in a bar in Renton. They agreed and the meeting was set up. Jerry had gotten the serial number off one of the most expensive guitar, a Stratocaster. Armed with that information they told the men that they were looking for a Stratocaster and did they have one? The man said they would check. When they met, Jerry and Ted had a way of bumping a person as though it was accidental to pat them down to see if they were armed. They found out that the high jackers were not armed. At first Jerry acted as though he only wanted the guitar and a few pieces. After extensive negotiations they agreed upon a tentative price dependent upon inspection and inventory. The men refused to "piece meal" it and said all or nothing. The four of them went on a short drive to an old commercial parking lot in Seattle. They got to the truck and looked through it and found the Stratocaster. It was the stolen one with the same serial number. The men were asking $50,000.00 for the whole load.

They went into a nearby building and dickered. Jerry and Ted knocked them down to $40,000.00. Jerry showed them a wad of money and told them where they wanted the semi delivered and then went back to the truck. The two men got in and were ready to drive out. Jerry jumped on the driver's side boards and Ted on the other side, with their arms in the windows. Jerry said "I've got some bad news, some good news and some more bad news." The two looked really worried, "First the bad news, we've got guns." the men went white. Jerry said "The good news is we aren't going to shoot you." They brightened up, but the passenger said "Aww, what's the other bad news?" "Well, the last bad news is that we aren't going to shoot you because we are cops." The passenger looked at the driver and said "I fuckin' told you so." They gave up without a fight and Jerry and Ted got everything back to the band.

The band was able to get it all together and had their concert on time. They were so thankful they kept trying to slip Jerry and Ted tips, but they wouldn't take anything. These officers had a strict code of ethics and would never take any kind of gratuity.

* * * * * * * * * * * * * *

Detective Jorgenson was called in to his boss's office. Sergeant Ruffent had special plans for him. Jerry had been working as a detective for some time now and Ruffent knew he was a member of the organized crime investigation unit. Ruffent felt he would be the right man for what he had in mind. Jerry walked into the one man office to find Ruffent standing by the window behind his desk. Ruffent was a big man, 6'4", medium built, slightly plump, wore glasses, had a friendly smile, and an easy going temperament. He was dressed in dark slacks, with a light blue shirt and a conservative tie. He was a man that didn't get overly excited about things. He liked his Vodka martini, and was considered a ladies man. He used to run the narcotic division.

There wasn't much to see, in the office an old fashioned oak desk, reclining chair, assorted file cabinets and a wall of book cases that held more photos than books.

There were two others in the office as well. Captain Miller and Major Rockford were standing in front of the filing cabinets. Ruffent stubbed out his cigarette in a rather plain glass ashtray sitting beside the calendar on his desk. As Jerry entered Ruffent indicated that he should take the only other chair, a stiff wooden model near the desk. Jerry was wondering what was going on. It was one thing to be called in to go over case information with Ruffent but what were the other two here for? He couldn't think of any problems he had come up against that might get the attention of the upper brass. He assumed he would find out shortly.

All three men began firing questions at Jerry. First of all, asking about his marriage situation. Jerry confirmed what they already knew, that he was separated. Next they wanted to know if he felt that he could get away for extended periods of time. Jerry had to pin them down there. How long was "an extended period of time" and so forth. They stated that it should be between one to three months. They wanted to know how he felt about associating with a rough crowd. Then they asked if he ever smoked marijuana? He said "Hey, I went to college." Would he smoke it again if he had to? They knew that he had been a professional dirt bike rider, but could he handle a street bike?'

Now it finally came out. They were looking for a member of the organized crime investigation unit to infiltrate an outlaw motorcycle club to see if the gang was involved in organized crime.

They went on to say that they had an informant who could introduce him to the gang. The department would also work up a phony rap sheet for him if he agreed. They wanted him to let his beard and hair grow out to get ready to play the part. Jerry was intrigued. It sounded like a challenge and maybe even a little fun. He agreed and they began briefing him further.

Over the next few weeks, he was to purchase special boots, a chain and wallet, gloves, helmet, a leather jacket, chaps and other gear. Next, the department sent him to the Canadian border to find the parts they needed to put a bike together for him. It seems that the border patrol confiscated several bikes involved in smuggling drugs. The department was able to get enough parts, with no identifying numbers or markings to build an outlaw bike for him.

On his way to the border Jerry began thinking about the questions put to him. He felt no threat at all about becoming involved with the type of people in the gang. He chalked that up to his up-bringing.

* * * * * * * * * * * * * *

Jerry was the youngest of six, raised in a 30' trailer. His dad was a steam fitter and traveled all over the country wherever the company sent him. Jerry was born in Salem then they moved to Astoria, Oregon. Next stop was Camp Hanford nuclear reservation where he learned to swim in the warm water of the nuclear plant outlet. Next they moved to Paducah, Kentucky.

On their way to their next stop in Kansas, pulling the 30' trailer with a 6 cylinder 49' Studebaker pick-up truck they had an accident.

The roads there were a series of dips and hills with creeks and culverts at the bottom of each dip. As his dad approached the bottom of one dip, two cars, passing each other and heading straight for him came over the next hill and bore down on them. His dad swerved to miss the cars and the wheels of the pickup dropped into the culvert. The right front wheel hit the culvert and came up through the floor-boards breaking his mother's foot. Jerry and his sister, riding in the back were thrown out. His sister was thrown clear and broke her arm but the truck rolled over and on top of Jerry. Fortunately the ditch was muddy and he was pushed down into the mud. Everyone was looking for him for some time, and could not find him. He had been unconscious but came to and called out. It took several people to roll the truck off of him. Thanks to the saturated ground he suffered only a few scratches and bruises.

The next location was in Missouri, then Sunnyside, Washington and back to Hanford. Later, they moved to West Richland, Bellingham, Washington and finally back to Salem, Oregon.

Jerry's youngest sister Barbara was born with a birth defect and whenever they went to a new school kids would pick on her. There was always one guy that would pick on her and it was up to Jerry to defend her. Although he was "the baby" of the family, he was big for his age and he soon made it clear that no one was to mess with his sister. Even though they argued and squabbled among themselves, he wouldn't let anyone else hurt her.

Whenever they started a new school he learned it was easier just to go right up to the biggest meanest guy in school and when that guy started a fight Jerry would knock the crap out of him. Then he had no other problems. He learned to handle himself at a young age.

He was often "expelled" for being in a fight even though the principal knew that he never started them. The principal would tell him that he knew he was just defending himself but since he expelled the other boy, Jerry would have to take a day off also. In spite of everything Jerry was the only male in the family that graduated from High School.

What it all boiled down to, was that Jerry had been fighting tough guys most of his life. So what was the big deal with a few bikers? At 6'4"and 240lbs., Jerry didn't have too many challengers to worry about.

When he was 18, he had a date with a girl whose dad was very strict and said that if his daughter was not in by 12:00pm he would be in big trouble. On the way home, Jerry's car broke down. He was really worried about getting her home on time and was hoping to borrow a car somewhere. Every house he looked at was dark. Then as he was walking along the sidewalk he noticed a car parked with the keys inside. No one was around, so he borrowed the car with every intention of returning it as soon as he got his date back home.

When he drove back and parked the car where he found it the police were waiting for him, and he was arrested. They were not impressed with his story. When he went before the judge the judge said "Well son, since this is your first offence, I will give you your choice. You can go to jail, or join the service and serve your country". Jerry replied, "Anchors away your honor."

In boot camp, the guys were all griping about how hard everything was. Jerry said "You know guys, I don't know what you are complaining about. You get three meals a day, the foods not at all bad. I have my own bed for the first time in my life, and the drill sergeant is nicer than my dad ever was."

Jerry had worked his way up to an E4 in the Navy and wanted to train for a better position. He was going to Yeoman school in San Diego, California. He married a girl he knew in high school when he went on leave in Seattle. After he graduated from Yeoman School he was transferred to U.S. naval schools Command at Treasure Island in San Francisco where he worked for the Commander. He was working curriculum and training aids. Their son Paul was born there, ten months later.

Jerry had always wanted a motorcycle. One day he saw an ad in the local paper for a Honda 250 Scrambler. It was for sale in a little town about 60 miles away. His wife went with him and he bought it. Jerry had never ridden a motorcycle before so he spent about ten minutes riding around the neighborhood getting familiar with the bike then headed back to San Francisco. He rode the bike whenever he had time from his Navy job. About 4 months later he found out about a flat track club nearby. He rode his bike over and watched the races. He really enjoyed that and decided that he would like to try it.

One of the guys in the flat track club had a 500 Triumph for sale. Jerry traded his Scrambler and $200.00 for it. The bike was not street legal, so he rode back home through the back streets. The only place he had to store the bike was on the back deck of his house. To get there he had to ride up 10 steps to the front porch, make a 90 degree turn, then through the living room to the back porch.

The following Saturday he went to the flat track and practiced with the guys in the race club. He had a great time, so he joined the club. He started racing every Saturday. Jerry didn't have a trailer to haul his bike. It was not street legal so to get to the track he had to ride the back streets and hope he wouldn't get caught. One Saturday he was running late and the traffic was bumper to bumper. He couldn't get around the cars so he was riding down the shoulder. He came to a curve and as he rounded it, there was a cop who had pulled a car over. The cop was standing on the shoulder side of the car because of the heavy traffic. Just behind the cop was a deep ditch. Jerry had nowhere to go, so he just blew by, in-between the cop and the car. That cop was really surprised. It all happened so fast he didn't have time to react. He was really angry.

The next Saturday there were two motorcycle cops waiting for him by the curve. The second they saw him coming they started after him. Jerry dove down into the ditch, up the other side and across a field and took off into a housing track. He found an open garage door, dove in and shut the door. The motorcycle cops didn't catch him. From then on, he rode the back streets part way to the track then got off the bike, turned the engine off and walked it down the hill leading to the track, sitting side saddle. If he saw a cop, he just stood up and pretended he was walking the bike.

Jerry raced for about a year and seldom won. He did run consistently in 4th or 5th place though. He did win a few heats and just enjoyed the sport. He said it was a great way to relive stress. About a year after he joined the club, one of the members who was an Air Force Reservist went on a training mission to Spain. While there he went to watch the motocross races. He got really excited about this type of racing and took 16m.m. movies of the action. When he got back to the U.S. he showed the movies to the club. Everyone really liked it and thought it was cool. Some of the members were rich enough to go out and buy a motorcycle they could use on a motocross track. There were only two companies in the U.S. that made bikes that could really be used for motocross at that time one was a CZ and the other a Maico. Jerry really wanted one of those bikes but there was no way he could afford it. He was still in the Navy and working part time for the Commander. He got a job working three nights a week as a bouncer in a Country Western Bar at the fishermen's terminal. His navy buddy worked there as well.

He finally was able to get a motocross bike. It was a 250cc, 2-stroke CZ. It was surprisingly heavy compared to his other bike. Jerry was also on the Navy football team and was not able to race every weekend but was out there whenever possible.

One night there were a couple of black men who were causing a lot of trouble at the bar. Jerry and his partner asked them to leave. They refused so the bouncers threw them out. They came back a second time and wanted to fight and were roughed up and thrown out again. They came right back in with clubs. Jerry and his partner subdued them and threw them out for the third time with instructions not to come back. After the bar closed they were walking out to their motorcycles when a black car came roaring by and the men were shooting at them. Jerry decided to quit.

The motorcycle club members who weren't working would find a pasture to rent for the weekend. Preferably one with hills. The members would meet there and practice their motocross skills. Soon, other clubs started showing up and wanted to race. It wasn't long until the other clubs would also rent a pasture and hold races. That way the clubs could go to a different location each weekend and race and didn't have to rent their own pasture as often. The clubs started charging a entry fee and getting trophy's. Jerry won his first trophy at one of these meets.

Two years later their second son Pete was born. Jerry was really proud of the boys. Whenever he could find a way the family would go with him. He didn't want to miss out on any of their growing up. They were riding their own bikes when they were four years old.

In those days, the bikes didn't really go fast enough to cause any serious injuries. Although Jerry crashed a lot and bought a lot of handle bars he was never badly hurt. He continued to race for the next eight years, although his wife was not happy about it. The sport of motocross took off and more and more races cropped up all over the country. Jerry spent every weekend he could racing.

*   *   *   *   *   *   *   *   *   *   *   *   *   *

Jerry had been thinking about how cramped his family was in their trailer. He often thought that it would be great, to somehow have extra room, but still be able to move the trailer.   During his time in the service, he came up with an idea for a room that could be pulled out when parked then pushed back when a person needed to move the trailer. When he got out of the Navy he decided to put his idea to work.   He first made a scale model of his "Expando Room".   He then hired a patent attorney to submit his idea to the patent office.   When he got his patent they drew it all up, made a pamphlet that showed pictures of the Expando Room and the details about it. Then he hired a salesman.

Jerry took his brother Fred in as a partner and they met Sam when he applied for the job.   Sam was in his late 50s, immaculately groomed, gray hair, 5'9" about 150 pounds. He was intelligent and very friendly. Jerry liked him right away.   Sam was excited about the project and kept saying, "This is really cool. I can definitely sell this." They sat down and discussed it and came up with a base price for the unit.   Then discussed what they should charge for extras.   Things like extra windows, sliding doors, different kind of metal for roofing or siding etc. They decided that Sam would earn 20% of the gross price.   Then Sam left, in his Cadillac to sell Jerry's idea. Sam sold four units the first week.

After four months, Sam wanted to buy into Jerry's business. Sam was selling the units faster than they could build them.   They decided that 5% of all his earnings would go toward buying into the company.   Sam spent a lot of time selling units in the Portland area and they got a lot of their supplies from that area. Consequently Jerry wanted Sam to pick up supplies on his way back.   The only problem was that since they were a new company they had not yet established credit accounts with the supply companies. They needed to pay cash. By this time they trusted Sam completely and decided that they could put his name on the bank account so that he could write checks for supplies.

Everything went great for about three months.   It was pay day for their employees. Jerry went to the bank to set the payroll up and found out there was only $20.00

in the checking account. Two days before that Sam and come in and drawn $100,000.00. The bank claimed that they had tried to call both Jerry and Fred but they had not answered so they allowed the withdrawal. They never saw Sam again. They turned it in to the police department, but they said it was a civil problem. They finally got the prosecutor's office to issue a warrant, but Sam was long gone. Jerry and Fred had to lay off their four employees and the secretary. They had two units that were completed and they sold them, one of their trucks and some of their tools to pay the wages due the employees as well as their suppliers. Then they let their lease on the building go and moved everything else into their Dad's barn. They set up shop there and Jerry and Fred built two more units. They were finished and ready to deliver. That same night, their Dad who now had Alzheimer's, came into the barn and turned on a heater that was set aside because it wasn't working properly. He went off and left it going. The barn caught on fire and destroyed everything. Not only the two finished units, but all their tools and the last truck. Time to give up. In the past another company had tried to buy Jerry's patent, so he contacted them and made a deal. The offer was less now, but he took it anyway.

Then Jerry went to work as a heavy construction laborer for the next five months. That winter when he was between jobs he saw an ad in the paper that drew his interest. It said "Correctional Officers needed. Oregon State Penitentiary." He answered the ad and took the test at 8:00 the next morning. They scheduled an interview at noon. He took the physical and at 4:00pm they gave him a uniform and by 8:00pm he worked his first shift.

Jerry tried to treat the inmates as fairly as possible but some of the other guards were really rough on them. One in particular, Ralph, who was 6' 5" and about 320 pounds, none of which was fat, would often slap them and shove them around. He would write them up, even if they did not do anything and they would lose privileges and sometime be put in the hole. He was also rude to the other officers. A real ass hole. The inmates hated this man with a passion.

In March of '68 there was a major riot. Jerry and 26 other officers were taken hostage. They were tied up and had to sit against a wall. When they were first captured the inmates would gang up on the officers and were beating them. Several were pounding on Jerry when some of the other inmates came and pulled them off. One of them said "Hey, leave him alone, he is one of the good guys." They were not gentle with Ralph at all. In fact after they beat him unconscious, they scalped him. A head wound produces a lot of blood. After 12 hours, the inmates that were running the riot became concerned that if Ralph died it would hurt their ability to negotiate.

They wanted someone to take him out. Jerry was the only one big enough to carry him and he had always treated them well. They asked him if he would do so and of course he agreed. He carried Ralph out and turned him over to the medics. They had Jerry go into a room where he was debriefed for four hours.

Jerry and the remaining officers were working 12 hours a day, 7 days a week. This went on for 2 and a half months. With all the overtime Jerry earned enough to buy the commercial fishing boat he had always wanted. Then he quit, as well. Meanwhile, while he was still working at the prison his third son Perry was born. Jerry was thrilled. He also knew that he needed to get work as soon as possible to support his growing family. He was still racing his bike on the weekends and whenever possible.

That summer he went commercial fishing for Salmon out of Coos Bay, Oregon and fished between Newport and Tillamook. Or. In the fall he worked at his construction job. At night he attended college on the G.I. bill. His goal was to be a lawyer.

The following spring he told the foreman that he wanted to take off and go fishing for the summer. His boss said "Tell you what; I will make you a deal. I will give you the time off if you promise to come back for big concrete pours." Jerry agreed and spent a second summer commercial fishing. The following fall, he sold his boat then went back to his construction job and to college. Meanwhile he was building a larger boat, for fishing.

The only time that he did not continue racing his bike was when he was out fishing. He improved steadily and was a lot more confident.

The company that Jerry's wife worked for moved to Seattle. The company helped them buy a home in that area. His wife moved to Seattle, but Jerry was still in college, so he stayed in Salem and worked construction while going to school nights.

After he got his Bachelor's degree, he decided that it was just taking too darn long to try to work and go to school part time at night. So, he quit his job, moved to Seattle and went to law school full time, on the G.I. bill.

When he got to the Seattle area motocross racing had gone professional. He was able to qualify and started racing every weekend. He was able to get a new bike. It was a '69 Penton. That company later became "KTM" It was a 250 cc that he bought while he was still working construction. He had also been able to purchase a used van to haul his bike. Money was tight by then, so he had a cheap pit with little in the way of equipment. He finally qualified to enter a big race. This was one of the preliminary races for the Nationals at Puyallup, Washington. Jerry raced a four race series on Saturday and Sunday. He finished fourth overall.

There was an older, nicely dressed man, hanging around Jerry's pit. At one point he said pointing to Jerry's rear tire, "Little hard to get traction with that, isn't it?" Jerry answered, "You gotta race what you got." The man just laughed and left. When the race was over Jerry was loading his bike in his van when the man came back. He gave Jerry his card and said he was the owner of University Honda/Bultaco. Jerry saw the name Ben Calder on the card.

He was 6' 2" about 230 pounds a little pudgy, defiantly not the athletic type, in his mid-40s, but nicely dressed and well groomed. Ben said "Come on in during the week and talk to me." Jerry replied, "Mister, I am going to school all week long. If you want to talk you have to do it now." He laughed again. "You are direct, I'll give you that. I would like to give you a trial. I'd like to give you a Bull 250. I'll give you a jersey, keep up the bike, $50.00 for each time you race to cover gas and the entry fee. You keep all the prize money. I'll give you a month.

I want you to race Wednesday night and Sundays. After that we'll see how you're doing.   I am not giving the bike to you, just loaning it. You will have to do your own wrenching, but I'll pay for parts and machining." Jerry wasn't sure he really believed all this, but he said "Sounds like a damn good idea to me. I'll be down on Monday night to pick up the bike." Ben said "No, I need to prep a bike. Give me until Wednesday". Now Jerry was sure he was full of shit. Ben wanted him to race on a bike he never rode before the same night he picked it up? So, Wednesday afternoon as soon as he got out of school Jerry went to the shop. He walked inside and told the lady at the desk that he was there to see Ben. She looked at him and smiled, then said in a very sweet voice. 'Oh, you must be Mr. Jorgenson. Ben is expecting you." Jerry was finally starting to believe this was for real. She took him up stairs to Ben's office.

Ben welcomed him and as soon as he sat down, gave him three jerseys with his name on them and the Bultaco motto on the front.   Ben went over the terms that he spoke of at the race track and had Jerry sign a contract that he would give the bike back and understood it was a loner. Ben then took Jerry downstairs and introduced him to his parts man who asked, "What size shoes do you wear and what is your pants size?" Jerry told him and he rummaged around, then tossed Jerry a box with a new pair of motocross boots. Then gave him a pair of leathers and said "Here try these on." Jerry looked at Ben and asked, "Do I have to give these back too?" Ben said "No they're yours. Who would want them after your sweaty ass has been in them?"

Ben then took Jerry back and introduced him to Greg. Greg was a slim guy in his late 20s, about 5'8", a real working man. He was Ben's head mechanic. Greg turned around and pointed and said "There she is." Jerry was blown away. That bike was frickin' gorgeous. It gleamed like a diamond. They loaded it in his van. Jerry went to pick up his wife and kids and they went to Puyallup about 35 miles away.

As it turned out, the starter at the race track was a friend of Jerry's. Jerry explained that it was a new bike that he had never ridden. He asked the starter if he would let him out to ride the whole time that the practice series was going on. His friend said that as long as he didn't show boat or make a spectacle of himself and kept it low key, he could probably let him do so.

His biggest concern was that other riders might think Jerry was getting special treatment. Jerry agreed and stayed out on the far end of the track from the practice starts. He would wait until they all passed him then chase after them. He did get one chance to practice the start. He really wasn't sure if it would be best to start in first or second gear.

In the past he had consistently been between 4th to 6th position out of the first corner. Then he had to race his ass off to finish well. So he really needed to get the feel of the new bike.

The first race came up and when the flag dropped he launched and dove into the first corner. Dirt was flying off the front wheel and it was digging into the curve. The Penton never could do that. After the first curve going up grandstand hill it dawned on him that there was no one else around him. At the top of the hill he got a lot of air and was having a ball. After three laps he came around a curve and there was Ben standing at the side of the curve.

Jerry was bouncing off the curve using the wall as a berm. Ben had both arms spread wide, his mouth wide open and a huge smile on his face. Jerry won that race hands down. Ben was thrilled. He came over to Jerry's pit and said "That was pretty good. Now let's see how you do in the next one."

Jerry thought "Wow, the way this things corners I can go anywhere. The power is phenomenal!"

After the second race Ben said "You drop by the shop every time you win. I'll throw a new knobby on there." On Thursday night, Jerry went by and Ben had a new tire put on the bike. Greg had a grand master plan. He said "If I move the top of the rear shocks forward two inches and the bottom of the rear shocks back two inches, replace the shocks with longer ones and put a heaver spring on them, then reverse and extend the front forks, you'll have an extra three inches of travel all around."

This would increase the speed and improve the handling. This of course would take a lot of machining and welding to make it happen. Jerry thought that Greg was having as much fun as he was, trying out his new ideas. Greg worked a lot of over time to get it done by

Saturday noon, so Jerry could race on Sunday. He was just tightening the last bolt when Jerry came to pick it up.

He took it out to a gravel pit to try it out. It sat a little higher but OH MAN did it handle well. He raced Sunday and won both motos. Jerry was winning every race. There was a thirteen week race series. If someone won them all he got extra prizes. Jerry kept on winning. While he was earning enough to make it all worthwhile it wasn't enough to live on. It was then that he got a job, selling R.V,s on Monday, Tuesday, Thursday and Friday evenings from 4 p.m. to 10 p.m. and Saturday for 12 hours. He continued racing on Wednesdays and Sundays. He always took the family as they enjoyed it and it was a way to stay together. He continued his schooling during the days. This was an era when it seemed that everyone wanted an R.V. Jerry was doing very well and sold a lot of them He was earning 20% to start then it was raised to 25%.

Jerry was finishing up his studies needing just two more credits to get his Law Degree. A police officer from King County who was a class mate, taking a criminal law class, talked him into going out riding with him a few nights. Then the officer talked Jerry into taking the test to become an officer. Jerry said he wasn't interested in becoming a police officer

His friend said "Why not try it? It is good experience to take different tests. It's on Saturday so get off your ass and give it a try just for the heck of it." Jerry decided to take the day off from the R.V. sales and take the test. The test was similar to a S.A.T. test and since Jerry was doing well in school he aced it. Then he took the physical, agility test and the psych test. They were from one to two weeks apart. He was surprised when he not only passed the tests, but was called to interview for the job. One of the interviewers, a mean looking, 6 foot 5 inch veteran Captain, got right in Jerry's face and said "Are you sure working with these big bad criminals won't scare you?" Jerry stood right up to him face to face and said "I don't scare easy, ass hole." The Captain said "I like this guy." He got the job.

He only intended to keep the position for about a year, then take the bar exam. 20 years later, he still hadn't taken the bar.

*   *   *   *   *   *   *   *   *   *   *   *   *   *

One day, while working his shift, a call came in asking for help with a loose monkey. There was no animal control then and they did not have portable phones to call for back-up so each officer was on his own. They had to be able to handle all kinds of situations themselves. Jerry responded to the call and the address was way out in the country at the end of a cul-de-sac. There were two houses there, one big and one small. A woman came rushing out of the small house screaming "They went that way. They went that way!" pointing toward the Snoqualmie river bottom.

Jerry headed down the slope carrying a animal catch stick. He could see fresh foot prints in the soft flooded sandy river bottom. As he was walking down through the brush he heard a shot and a guy came running up the hill, saw Jerry and ran toward him yelling, "Give me your gun, quick, give me your gun!" Jerry thought, "That ain't gonna happen" and hollered back, "NO!" The guy was carrying a shot gun and said "I hit it in the face with the 4\10 but only had one shell. Throw that stick away, he will kill you with it then kill me." Then he showed Jerry the scars on his body and said that is what the animal did to him last time it got out. He said he was the animal's sole owner and gave Jerry permission to shoot it. In fact he practically begged him to shoot it. He said he ran a primate research center and had two animals. One was castrated the other wasn't. It was the one that escaped. He said it got out two years ago and almost killed him. He recaptured it and got a larger stronger cage but now he was out again. Jerry couldn't help wonder what he was doing to the animals under the guise of "research". .

They walked down toward the river and Jerry could see the animal squatting by the river bent down in a tight ball. It didn't look all that big or bad to him. It had blood on its face and one eye was shot out. He could tell it was in a lot of pain. He actually felt sorry for it.

Jerry started to walk toward it and the guy was almost crying, pleading, "Don't do that. Don't do that! Stay back!" Then it stood up. "OH SHIT!" It was a 5' 3" gorilla. He threw the stick down and drew his gun (a

357 Colt Python, 6" barrel with 175 grain jacketed shells). The gorilla took two steps toward him and he shot it twice in the chest. It stepped back then started toward him again. He put two more shots in it's chest, it rocked back then came forward again. This time Jerry shot lower into it's stomach. It went down, landing on one elbow holding its stomach and Jerry was then able to shoot it in the head to kill it. He told the guy that he was responsible for the body and needed to take care of it right away.

Jerry then went back toward his car and met with the woman that had called it in. She met him at the door and showed him her house. The gorilla had pushed in the door and she had run for the bathroom and locked herself in. The gorilla then tore up the entire house and left but did not try to get to her. She was extremely upset and thankful that it was dead.

* * * * * * * * * * * * * *

In late '72, Ben came to Jerry and said Honda was coming out with a new 2 stroke race bike. It would be a whole new step forward in moto cross bikes. He was going to get 2 before any other dealer in Washington and no one else would get one for 3 months. He wanted Jerry and Dave Winters, another winning rider, to ride as a race team. Dave was a wiry 5' 9" about 145 pounds with a heck of a sense of humor. He was always teasing someone. He was something of a ladies man. He got a little miffed when Jerry beat him, and his girlfriend would rag on him when that happened. Otherwise he was a great guy and a good rider. Ben said he would supply a deluxe trailer with logo, and awnings, chairs with the logo, jerseys and anything else they needed. Jerry really didn't want to do it as it seemed like a lot of work without much benefit to him. Ben told him that the Bultaco was not his priority and he needed to promote the new Elsinore. If Jerry didn't want to race the Elsinore he would have to take the Bull back.

Dave was all for the deal and really excited. Jerry didn't have a heck of a lot of choices so they made the deal. Jerry and Dave took delivery of the package on Saturday and drove to a small track east of Monroe. They could practice there for $5.00. Those bikes were FAST! They had a narrow power band and they had to keep the RPMs up but boy were they fast, a lot faster than they were used to. When it came time to head to the race track they were to get there early, pick the closest pit to the grandstand, park the trailer where everyone could see all the advertising and stay by trailer with the bikes on stands under the awning, nice and clean. They were to be there to talk to people and answer questions about the bikes whenever they were not on the track. Greg would be going as well and would be wrenching between mottos, while Jerry and Dave were talking to people. They had to wear those God awful bright jerseys as well.

Dave was faster than Jerry but not as consistent. Jerry actually won more races, but Dave was right there as well. They both really liked the bikes although they didn't corner as well as the Bull. They had to climb up on the gas tank to corner and were constantly moving around on the bikes. It was a lot more work then the Bull. They were however a lot faster. You could even go down, get back up and still win. After three races the knobby was shot and had to be replaced.

Jerry was still working as a beat cop while racing. After three months of winning all their races Ben said that he had over 53 orders. He attributed it to them. At the end of the three months, Ben came up with a plan. He wanted Jerry to run a motocross team. He was going to build a trailer that would hold 14 bikes with a storage area that would hold gas tanks, tools, tires, rims, handle bars, a welder and etc. They would cover all classes, mini, 250 cc and open. Jerry said he would do it but did not want to continue riding in the 250. He wanted to ride 360 open classes. Ben agreed. He said that Greg would go to all the races as well. Ben had a few riders in mind and so did Jerry. Jerry knew a kid named Rick Star. He was 14 and had been racing minis and was ready to move up. This kid was real National material.

They formed the team and started hitting all the tracks. With all the flashy advertising on the trailer, and clothes and the fact that they were wining more races all the time, it soon got to the point that the tracks were paying them a "show-up fee," to cover their expenses and their entry fee. Their whole pit was bright and professional. It was also very cool to have a mechanic meet you at the end of a race and walk your bike to the pit and work on it.

Jerry's wife was not at all happy about this as he would take his vacation from work to go racing. He was also racing cross country races now. One race in particular, The Dessert 100 that was run twice a year, was a race that Jerry really wanted to win.

The first time he raced it the temperature was close to 100 degrees. He collapsed the rear shocks during the first 50 miles. He took it to the pit to be fixed and while Greg was putting on new shocks Jerry chugged-a-lugged 32 oz. of ice cold Gator aid. He jumped on the bike and took off. He didn't make 5 miles and was on his hands and knees puking his guts out. You do not drink ice cold drink when you are that hot.- - He was so sick he could barely get back to the pits.

Six months later he rode the Elsinore in this same race. All the bikes would be lined up across the dessert and the bikes were propped up with sticks. The riders had to walk back 50 feet. Way off in the distance a smoke bomb was set off. The riders would run to their bikes, start them up and take off. This time Jerry placed 104 out of 1200 riders.

The next time, 6 months later, he tried again. This time he finished in 23rd place out of 1200 entries. The next time he talked Ben into letting him enter the Bultaco and he placed sixth.

Ok, one more time. Ben agreed to let him enter the Bull again. There were check points along the 100 miles and each bike had a card wired to the handlebars that had to be punched at each check point. When he went through the final check point the guy slapped him on the back and said that 2nd place was 12 minutes behind him. That was a pretty good feeling. After he left that check point, the course dropped down from the hills and he could see the sparkling of the rigs around the finish line about 10 miles away. It was a decent ride with powder sand and small knolls about 700' apart. Jerry is cruising along about 70 mph, just enjoying the heck out of himself. He was not really pushing top speed. All of a sudden the engine seized.

Jerry could not believe it. Only about 2 miles to go, in the lead for the first time and the bike quits. He jumped off and started pushing it. He still came in 3rd overall! He told himself that God does not want him to win this race.

24

Rick and Jerry decided to try one more time and ride as a team. He and Dave rode the Bultaco and won first place. They were 15 minutes ahead of all the others in their class. Jerry and his team continued to race until 1975,

Ben wanted Jerry to race a new production 360 Bultaco prototype. Jerry took it down to test it but it was blubbering coming out of the corner and Greg said he saw blue smoke. It was running too rich. Greg decided to reduce the jet from a 500 to a 360. He did all the work.

Jerry went out for the first race and smoked everyone at the first corner. He was hauling ass and when he came up to grand stand hill, got a lot of air. He was heading down the straight away to the tunnel hill. He tried to back off the throttle but the rpm didn't drop. The throttle stuck. He actually stripped the threads out of the brake rod. He was trying to reach the kill switch to shut the engine off with no luck. He went up and over the tunnel and went flying. Usually when you got air over the tunnel hill you landed about 40 feet then in the next 25 feet there was a sharp turn to the left. Jerry didn't land until he was past the curve. He landed hard bent the handle bars down and collapsed the whole bike. Something locked the front end and the bike took an endo, rear end over tea kettle then sailed over the chain link fence at the curve and was totaled. Jerry did not make it over the fence and crashed into it.

He knew he was badly hurt when he couldn't feel his legs. The ambulance stationed there, got to him in minutes, but his wife and kids were there first. They were all visibly upset. The medic team got him on a pack board and rushed him to the hospital. His family following close behind. He was x-rayed and told he had five broken bones, including his tail bone. The doctor told him he would get the feeling back in his legs when the trauma to his tail bone wore off. He was given pain meds and spent the night in the hospital. In the morning the doctor came in and told him that he did not have five broken bones. He had eleven broken bones and seven of them were ribs. He said that none were life threatening. He said the only one to worry about was his tail bone and that he needed at least two weeks of R & R from work and riding. Meanwhile Greg came in to see him and was really feeling badly. He said that the wreck was all his fault. He said that while working on the bike he had crimped the throttle cable. He didn't have any more cable and when he straightened it out, it seemed to be working so he thought it would be ok. It evidently wore during the race and failed.

When the police department found out he wasn't coming to work for two weeks they sent a legal representative who told him that the department could not afford to give him so much time off due to motorcycle injuries. He needed to decide if he wanted to race or be a policeman. Jerry agreed to quit racing but he hated to quit while he was down.

Six months later he started practicing again, on the sly. When the Puyallup 13 race series came up he started racing again. He won eleven of the thirteen. Of the two he lost, one was due to a broken rear rim and the other because of a blown transmission. Then he quit racing, as a winner.

*   *   *   *   *   *   *   *   *   *   *   *   *   *

For the next two months Jerry was involved with other cases. His hair was getting long enough to tie in a ponytail. His beard was longer and the tattoo he got in the Navy helped the look he was going for. This also gave him time to get to know the informant. According to Jerry this guy thought "He was sooo fuckin' smooth." Jerry did not trust him. He could have burned Jerry at any time. It was really an uncomfortable feeling.

Jerry started hanging out at the club bar. It was on the side of a hill overlooking the waterfront. It was a long, narrow building (about 90' X 30') in-between two industrial buildings. Not really a place where there was any other people services. It was a well-known biker bar and anyone else was discouraged from being there. A very large sign in the front read, "WE RESERVE THE RIGHT TO REFUSE SERVICE TO ANYONE." - - There was a low wall, with a large picture window with the name of the bar on it. A single oversized door was the only entrance. Below the bar on the lower side of the hill, was a butcher shop. Just inside the door to left were two booths with plain wooden benches and heavy tables. That was where the sentries hung out. They were on the lookout for drive-by, pigs and anyone near the bikes. The bikes were parked on the street in front. It was a four lane road that was busy with commercial traffic during the day but almost no traffic at night. The occasional Joe citizen would wander by and get a little close to the bikes. The sentries would bail outside and command, "DON'T FUCK WITH THE SCOOTS.". Joe citizen would leave quickly.

Inside, the bar ran about 30' along the south side. In back, there were liquor bottles on the top shelf, glasses on the next one and Bud on tap, in the front. The floors were scraped up wood floors and the other booths and stools were all in need of repair. There was a small raised area in the back, with two stuffed couches for the club hierarchy. The whole place was dingy and dirty and had a funky smell to it. There were two pool tables and old posters on the wall advertising local bands or events in no particular order and many with expired dates. The smoke hung in wispy clouds over the whole area.

Jerry ordered a Rainier and started playing pool. He was a pretty good player so while he won several times he made it a point to lose a few as well. He got involved in a few arm wrestling matches. He won his share but didn't try to win them all. He worn plain riding gear, with no patches or logo on it and parked his bike in front with the others.

He was just hanging around being seen and not getting into anyone's face or causing any trouble. It was similar to the way animals sized each other up. This went on for the next few visits over two weeks.

The plan was that the informant would be across the street with a pair of binoculars watching for just the right moment. When Jerry would be talking with certain club members, he would come in, talk to some of the members and look over at him and say, "Hey Jerry, what are you doing here?" He wanted it to seem as though he was surprised to see him. The members knew this guy as he often bought or sold dope to them. They really didn't trust him either. They asked him how he knew Jerry and he told them he sold him some "ludes."

The informant was a weasely, skinny dude, 5'7" with bad teeth, pock marked face, a high pitched whinny voice and long unkempt hair. It was as though personal hygiene was the least of his priorities. He had dirty fingernails and was missing two fingers on his right hand from injecting heroin into his hand and collapsing the blood vessels there. His eyes were never still, always bouncing around. Drove you nuts. You wanted to grab his head and hold it still.

Now the gang was sizing him up and started asking questions. They were trying to be coy about it asking them here and there while playing pool, but it was pretty obvious they were grilling him. - Did he have a job? - Yes, he was a janitor. Where did he work? For the Northland School district. Did he have a family? No. Then the questions got more invasive, Do you have an old lady? Do you have any brothers or sisters? How much do you owe on your bike? Etc. Jerry answered. "Hey man, it's really none of your business." He wanted to stand up to them without being confrontational. They needed to know they could only push him so far. One night, Doug, the master at arms, asked him who he rode with. Jerry answered that he was an independent. Doug said "Have you ever thought about riding with a club?". Jerry said "Yeah, but I never found one I liked". Doug said "Why is that?" Jerry answered, "I knew a guy who rode with the Jokers and he was a punk." Doug laughed at that.

After 6 or 7 visits, the informant came in again. This time on his own, he actually sold some drugs to the gang right in front of Jerry. What a jerk. Trying to show off. It got to the point that Jerry thought he could have done this easier without him.

The gang became friendlier. They knew his name, would shake his hand and as all bikers did, give him a brother's hug. Jerry bought a LOT of beer and that made him pretty popular.

Over a period of time, talking about his past, things began to progress. They said that a janitor didn't make much and Jerry said "Yeah, but it gives me more time to do my side stuff." They asked, "Oh yeah, what is that?" Jerry said "Just stuff.." After a while he pretended to be drunk and after repeated questioning, he pretended to let it slip. "I sold stuff to the spooks on the hill. They are a paranoid bunch and need stuff to make them feel safer. So I sold them a few pieces." "Where do you get them?" "From a dude, just a dude." They asked, "Does your dude have any heavy shit?" "Na, just shit that other people were selling. Nothing heavy, that would cause serious shit." "So how much do you trust these guys you are selling to?" "Not at all, those dudes would do you in a heartbeat." A couple of visits later, the V.P. said they were going on a putt down to Ashland and back and asked if he wanted to go along? It was considered an honor, so he went.

There was a club house down there and they all got drunk, except for the prospects. There were 4 or 5 of them and they had to wait, hand and foot on the members, guard the bikes and do security work. Jerry just hung around the fringes and enjoyed the party. There were a lot of old ladies, hookers and titty bouncers and the party lasted all night.

When they got back Jerry was invited into the club house. This was a two story older house in a residential area that needed paint and general TLC The yard was overgrown with weeds. Inside there were couches in every room. There was a big heavy wooden table that looked like you could get up and dance on it. There were several bulky roller chairs around the table. The kitchen was tacky and could have used a good cleaning. You wouldn't want to lay any food down. There were posters on the wall and military black out curtains on the windows. In the middle of the wood table was a tray with joints for anyone who wanted them.

The club V.P., Mac, was in his early 40s, 5'9", built like a fireplug. He had an attitude of authority, and was reasonably intelligent. He was missing a front tooth and it was hard not to stare at it. He came over and asked if Jerry enjoyed the trip. He said "Yeah, I had a great time." "What do you think about riding with us?" Jerry said "Yeah, I said I had a great time." "No, I mean what do you think about trying out for a prospect?" Jerry looked thoughtful, "I don't know, I have to think about it. I am doing pretty good on my own." "You'd do better with us." Jerry wondered, "Yeah, so why is that?" "Because you would always have someone to cover your back." "I don't know, what's it going to cost me?" "It really doesn't cost you anything. You would have to sign over the title to your bike, make it club property". Jerry said "Bull shit, I ride my own bike." "No, no man, we don't take your bike, you keep it, you ride it, it is just insurance, that you're not going to bop in and bop out and try to screw us." Jerry said "It's a big move, I gotta' think about it. Mac said "It a honor to be invited. I lot of the members like you, they think you are an upright guy." "I still have to think about it." Mac went on to say, "We hardly ever invite someone outright. The offer won't stay on the table long." Yeah, I know, but I still have to think about it." Mac said "Yeah, I guess that is a smart move."

Jerry was regularly reporting to his superiors and had a special hidden entrance to the administration building, then through an underground passage to the courthouse. They were pleased with his progress. They were developing a profile of the average one per center biker. Guys about 5'9", beard and/or facial hair, tattoos, a rough childhood, few friends, no family ties, usually been bullied in school. They were like lost souls looking for a place it fit it. They liked the brotherhood and the unity. All had a violent side and wouldn't back down. They believed in honor and respect among the members of the gang. (The American Motorcycle Ass. classifies 1% of rider gangs are outside the law.)

Jerry's boss said that he was going to have to be very careful, so that no one could claim entrapment. They also said he would have to quit coming in and report by phone or meet someone in the field from then on.

Jerry was then assigned a special prosecutor. Frank was a pretty sharp cookie. He spent a whole weekend with Jerry going over the case. What had been done, what had been said to whom and how they should approach it in the future. This had to be coming from them, not suggestions from Jerry. They went over everything piece by piece. Who did what to whom and so forth. Frank had a big chalk board and mapped out what each member did and said. He was very thorough. He was also ecstatic over the fact that Jerry hadn't just jumped in and was giving the impression that he may not even join. It made him seem more believable.

On Monday night, when Jerry went to the club, Mac asked if had been thinking about joining. Jerry said "Yeah and I have more questions. I don't want to give up my business. I worked too long and too hard to lose it. These are tweaky bastards who don't trust just anyone." "Understood, and what you do with that is your business. But, if the club helped you out at all they would expect a cut". "That's cool, but I am still nervous about signing over my scoot." "There is no getting around that, it is a hard and fast rule."

Then Mac started explaining all the benefits members get. He said "You always got someone to cover your back. You got the brotherhood that always takes care of you. If you chip in and do part of the work, you share in the profits." Jerry asked, "What profits?" "You aint the only dude doing business." Like he was bragging. Jerry said "What kinda money we talking about?" Mac laughed, "Enough to keep you in beer and pussy!" "I still don't like signing over my bike." Mac fired back, "HEY, I don't know why you're so worried about it, we could have taken it any time we wanted to.". Jerry said in almost a growl, "Someone would have died over that one." Mac just laughed it off. The rest of the evening they talked generalities and when Jerry started to leave Mac said "Next time we have to get serious, so think about it. You know, if you decide to become a prospect, the club has to witness you commit a felony. We know a cop can't commit a felony.

Did he really want to take the next step? Once he was in, that deep, he would have to be constantly on guard. He would need to watch every move he made and everything he said.

Jerry got to thinking about what got him into this situation in the first place. After all he never intended to be a police officer, a detective and for damn sure not in a job that would put his life at stake. When he joined, he only intended to keep the job for a year.   Funny how things worked out.

*   *   *   *   *   *   *   *   *   *   *   *   *   *

Chapter 2
Seven Years Earlier

After he passed all the tests, the written test, the physical agility and strength test, his medical physical and the physic test then the interview he was hired as a policeman, things just seemed to escalate. Ha!, Thinking back on the physic test he remembered one of the questions the psychologist asked him. He was evidently trying to see how Jerry would react to it. He asked. "What is your sexual preference?" Jerry answered, "Well, I prefer women, don't you?" Then the doctor asked, "Would you ever have sex with your mother?" Although Jerry was just a little bit taken back, he maintained a cool demure. "No, but I would have sex with your mother." He passed.

After he was hired he had a week to buy his uniform and equipment. The department gave him a list of what he needed and a letter of authorization and sent him to the uniform store. He was lucky, as he was one of the first hired and first to the store. He was therefore able to get everything he needed right away.   The list included, two uniforms, he was able to get a good deal on one used one, but had to buy the second one new, a gun, gun belt, holster, badge, handcuffs, mace, night stick, flash light, a pack of ball point pens, brief case that would hold a revised code book, a package of ticket books, traffic code book, rulers, pencils, chart compass, a 100' metal tape and a 25' metal tape, bullet pouches, stapler, paper clips, erasers, extra reports and paper work sheets, metal clip board and bullets.

The department did furnish your flash light batteries and practice bullets, but you had to buy your own duty bullets. Altogether, it set him back $4,500.00. Oh, and they did supply the car and shot gun. When Jerry picked out his gun, he got the biggest, nastiest gun in the case. It was a .357 magnum, Colt, Python, with a 6" barrel.

Jerry and seven others showed up at the court house at 8:00am the following Monday, and were sworn in then took a three hour indoctrination class. They filled out insurance forms, indicated next of kin, W4 forms and other paperwork. After a long lunch, they sat through several lectures from different commanders, and then they went home.

The next morning they were sent to Fort McKinley for an all-day fire arms course. The first couple of hours they were lectured on the shoot don't shoot/pyramid of force scenario. Steps necessary before you can use deadly force unless you are under fire. The instructor also told them what their personal liability was and what the department would back them on.

Next they went to the shooting range. While Jerry had handled guns and was an avid hunter, he had never shot a pistol before. He couldn't hit shit! He was pathetic. The instructor said "You are an insult to the Colt Firearms Company."

They shot until noon and Jerry did not improve. The instructor told the rest of them to break for lunch. As the rest of them left, he called Jerry back and handed him 500 rounds of ammo and said "I don't care if you're have to stay here until we get back, you're not going and you better be hitting the target by then." Then he got in his car and started to leave. Jerry said "Hey, wait a minute. Aren't you going to stay and watch me?" "Why should I? Are you going to lie to me?" Jerry said "No." "Then why do I need to be here?"

Jerry stayed until they got back two hours later. At one point, the base security guard came by and asked why he was still there. He answered "Because the instructor said I couldn't hit shit." The guard looked at the target and said "I can understand that."

34

By the time he had fired 200 to 300 rounds, he was hitting tight center mass. By the next 100 rounds he was right on and by the next 100 he was hitting triple "taps".

The next morning he was back at 8:00am with the rest of the rookies and started shooting. The instructor was watching. He said "Evidently those 500 rounds were not wasted. Jerry went on to rate in the top percentage of shooters and scored five perfect 300.

The next day they had hand to hand combat and night stick training. They also learned handcuff techniques. The following day they went to class to learn patrol procedure, how to park for traffic stops, how to park to conduct a felony stop and how to use their car for cover. It was good to get the weekend off, when that was over.

The following Monday they were at the court house and were assigned various shifts and precincts. They were then ordered to report to the precincts they were assigned to. When Jerry arrived he was given the basic tour, holding cells, interview room, locker room, Breathalyzer area etc. The building was an old abandoned World War 2 barracks that was partitioned off. He was told to report back in the afternoon, one hour early for his shift, to meet his Sergeant for indoctrination.

Sergeant Davidson, was a big man, 6' 3", slender and in good shape. He had gray hair and was in his 50s. He was always neat, well liked and very, very professional. The man had a lot of patience and stood by his men. The kind of man Jerry would like to be like. The first night he was to ride with a senior officer, the next night with a different officer and the 3rd night, the Sergeant threw him a set of keys and said "Go earn your money."

When Jerry first started, the only citation he was familiar with was, "Failure to use due care and caution." King County deputies were expected to be criminal investigation deputies. They were not expected or pressured into writing traffic citations. Jerry quickly developed the mentality of, "If you piss me off by your driving, I write you a ticket."

Jerry was on call to respond to citizens' complaints. He had been working for 2 or 3 days and got a call from dispatch, saying a citizen called in saying that her elderly neighbor had collapsed inside her locked house. Jerry, being young and aggressive sped to the area with sirens blaring and lights flashing! Raced right by the house with several neighbors standing outside giving him a bewildered look as he zoomed by. OOPS! He had to turn around at the end of the block and come back meekly embarrassed with lights and siren off.

The neighbors said she was on the floor. He went to the door and pounded on it while looking through the tall glass window next to it. He could see her lying in the hall. She tried to move, raised up on one elbow then her eyes rolled back and she collapsed back on the floor. The door was locked so he kicked it in. She wasn't breathing. Jerry stated mouth to mouth and she coughed and started to breath. He reached for the phone, but she stopped breathing again. He repeated mouth to mouth and when she responded again he dragged her to the phone and was finally able to call for an ambulance. He had to revive her several more times before the ambulance got there. In those days there were no EMTs, no medic units, no

911, no cell phones, no portable radios, no dog catchers, no back-ups and you were on your own and needed to know what to do in every situation.

The women had been wearing a very strong perfume and although he washed several times, he could not get the smell off. Part of the way through his shift, his sergeant met him at the car and said "Hey, you know that old lady you pumped up? She had hepatitis." Jerry threw up. His sergeant said "I didn't expect that. Hey man, I was just shitin' you, she was in a diabetic coma."

Jerry soon learned that folks would often be angry when he arrived because of the amount of time it took to respond. If the call was for a burglary, when the intruder was gone, barking dogs, loose animals or non-emergency, he had to first respond to the more pressing cases. He told these folks that he was sorry and didn't blame them for being angry. He understood why they felt violated. He began to carry 57 cents in his right pocket. When someone yelled at him and said "I am a taxpayer and I pay your wages. Why couldn't you get here sooner?" Jerry would reach in his pocket, pull out the 57 cents, hand it to them and say, "Here, this is what you paid for police protection this year. Now we are even. If you want better police protection, call the County council and God knows I am willing to have more help out here."

The average ratio of police officers to population was 1.83 officers to 1,000 citizens. King County had only .75 officers to 1,000. Hence the reason that all were one man units and back up was hard to get. North King County alone, was approximately 2,275 square miles and the graveyard shift had just four officers working it.

One night, about 2:00 am a citizen called in saying there was an ongoing neighbor dispute over a property line and he had just heard shots fired. Jerry responded as quickly as possible. It was about 30 miles away. As he neared the location the address was hard to find as it was a rural area and only mail boxes to go by. The caller had said to go past the big red barn and it was the third driveway on the left. It was a long driveway and as he neared the barn he saw, in his headlights, a guy standing with his back to him holding a rifle. He hit the man with the spot light and saw steam coming off the ground beyond him. He realized there was a body there. Jerry parked about 50 feet away. Once he saw the body he turned on the P.A. system, and told the man to drop the gun. The man did not respond. He stood frozen in place, not moving. There was no radio coverage as he was in a dead zone, so Jerry was unable to call for backup. In any case it would take over 40 minutes for help to get there. Jerry would have to move across 50' of open pasture to get to the man. It was a pretty tense situation. He snuck up behind the man and tackled him, taking the gun away and handcuffing him in one swift move. The rifle had only one spent casing in the chamber.

The man was laying there on the ground, face down, crying. Jerry went to the body and checked it. The shot had hit this man, in the left femur, blowing a hole out the back the size of your fist. He bled out and died. So, now what do you do? Who was in the house and how would they respond. Would they shoot at him? You have a crime scene and you can't leave it unsecured. You have a suspect on the ground crying, a dead body, murder weapon and all the evidence laying right there. So now what do you do? You have no phone, no radio contact, no one responding to your voice. "Hey" he shouted "Is anyone there, can anyone hear me?" No neighbor close by. Jerry put the suspect in the back of the car. He almost had to carry him. The man was sobbing uncontrollably and almost collapsing.

When the suspect was secured in the back of the car Jerry started walking toward the house. He got about two thirds of the way there when another police car rolled in. That officer was also responding to the call but had a lot further to drive. Dispatch had been trying to reach Jerry and when they couldn't, that made the second officer worried about him. He was hauling ass to get there and was going so fast he almost passed the drive way. Spotting Jerry's car he slid almost 100 yards then whipped into the driveway and came to a screeching halt at the scene.

The rule is, the first officer on the scene has control. Jerry told him to keep an eye on the suspect and the crime scene so he could go to the house to call it in. The suspect's wife answered the door, saw him and started to cry. She kept saying, "What happened, what happened?"

Jerry said he needed to use the phone. She said "I have to go out and see Jim." Jerry said "No, you have to stay in the house, police orders." Her crying woke up their two children, about six and seven years old who also started crying. Jerry said "I really need to use your phone." She pointed toward the kitchen. Jerry said "You stay here and take care of your kids." He got to the phone and called dispatch. He told them he needed the sergeant and homicide. He told them that the suspect was in custody and the scene was contained. Unknown to Jerry the women had come to the kitchen door and was listening. When he said he needed homicide she went ballistic and so did the children.

Jerry left the phone number and was waiting for a call back from his sergeant. When he did call Jerry told him what he had and what was being done. Jerry and the second officer were told to stay on the scene until the sergeant and the homicide detectives arrived.

* * * * * * * * * * * * * *

On one occasion, when Jerry was working swing shift he noticed a Crummy, a type of shortened school bus, converted to a four wheel drive, weaving all over the road. When he stopped it, it became apparent that the driver was drunk. He had him step out of the rig and Jerry administered the sobriety test. The man failed. There were eight loggers in the rig and according to them, they had been working on a broken rig and drinking beer all day. They were on their way to town for more beer.

As Jerry stated to handcuff the driver to arrest him, all eight of the loggers jumped him. He was getting his ass kicked. He was down on his hands and knees, the knees of his uniform ripped out, his shirt ripped off, his watch gone, his hat crushed and three of his teeth knocked out. He was just about to pull his gun and start shooting knee caps, when a second crummy pulled up and the loggers in that one jumped out and rescued him. Then they helped get the drunks back into the first crummy and tied them to the seats. He was in another dead zone, with no radio contact and no phone. He was furious, so he locked his patrol car and drove the crummy the thirty-five miles back to the jail.

It was unbelievable how eight rough tough loggers could turn into a bunch of whinny wimps in such a short time. All but one of them was whining, "Give me a break!" or, "I can't do this, I'll lose my job."

He drove around to the loading dock and asked a worker to call the jail and tell them he needed help to control the eight men he had in custody.

The jail sent down three officers, extra handcuffs and chains. They got them all cuffed and marched them into jail. Jerry got a lot of teasing about that. The guys all said "Don't fuck with Jorgenson, he'll arrest you and drive you to jail in your own car."

After Jerry got all the booking and paperwork done, he drove the crummy back the 35 miles to get his patrol car, then had the crummy impounded. - - One nice thing though, the county would reimburse him for the uniform and watch he lost while on the job. He did learn to use a cheap watch as they would only replace it with a cheap watch.

*　*　*　*　*　*　*　*　*　*　*　*　*　*

One event took place in the late evening. Jerry was dispatched to a family fight. A neighbor had called to say that there was awful screaming coming from next door. When Jerry got there, he too heard the screaming and pounded on the door. No one answered, so he "stuffed" (smashed) the door. As he entered he heard the screams coming from the kitchen. When he looked in, the man had the woman crammed in the corner, in a fetal position trying to protect herself, while he beat relentlessly on her. Jerry rushed in, grabbed the man by the hair, spun him around and dropped him face first to the floor.

He was kneeling on the man's back handcuffing him when the next thing he knew, the wife had stabbed him in the neck with a butcher knife. He stood up and hit her as hard as he could. She went down like a rag doll. He told the man to stay on the floor and grabbed the phone off the wall and called dispatch and shouted, "I need immediate help. I need back up and an ambulance for me. I've got a knife in my neck!" They said "Hang on, we will be right there." An officer was there in three minutes and his Sergeant was there before the ambulance arrived. They kept telling him to sit still and don't move. The knife was still in his neck. The ambulance attendants had him lay face down and they taped the knife and supported it in one position so that it would not move. They did not know how close it was to the carotid artery. They were very careful not to let it move. At the hospital, he was X-rayed, given pain medicine, then taken into surgery and the knife removed. The doctor stitched it up and Jerry had to stay the night, under observation. The next two days he was off his normal shift but then went back to work.

Jerry had been on the job about a year and a half, when he was assigned to a Sergeant Phil. Phil was a big man, 6' tall and well-muscled. He was in his mid-30s, had a mustache and receding, wispy brown hair. He wasn't one to pressure the men too much and most of them liked him. They did say he was a pussy hound though. The first thing he said to Jerry was that he didn't like him. He said "I heard of the work you guys did and I don't like it." Jerry said "Well, what does that mean? Do I have to watch my back all the time?" "No, just don't screw up here." Jerry knew what he was talking about. The officer he had been working with was a major screw up. His name was Fredrick and he was always saying and doing stupid things. He was a constant fucking embarrassment. A total hell to be around.

The last time Fredrick was with Jerry he kept begging to drive. Finally Jerry let him. A short time later while driving in heavy traffic a car was speeding toward them, weaving in and out of traffic and flashed by. Fredrick spun a U turn, barely missing several other cars and went after it. He was speeding in and out of traffic with several close calls and in hot pursuit. When the car finally pulled over he stopped behind it got out and went up to it. He was there for several minutes then came back and got in the patrol car.

Jerry thought he would be getting the ticket book. When Fredrick got back into the car the other car drove away. Jerry said "What the hell is going on? Why aren't you writing them a ticket?" Fredrick said "Naw, I couldn't, they were just too cute." Jerry was furious! He yelled "Get the fuck out of my car. Get the fuck out of my car!" and shoved him out the door. Fredrick frowned "Come on man, what's going on?" "You stupid son of a bitch. You endangered my life driving like that and you let them walk?" Jerry slammed the door and drove off.

It was three miles back to the station. Jerry parked in front and walked in. His commanding officer, Davidson, said "Oh shit, what did you do with Fredrick?" Jerry held up a finger, got on the phone to the dispatch supervisor and told him, "If Fredrick calls, say, Sorry, you're walking back".

Then he turned to Davidson and told him what happened. He went on to say that if he ever had to ride with Fredrick again he would probably kill him. Davidson said "Ok, go on back to work. I'll take care of it." Davidson was a good man to work for. The men respected him. He was a role model for Jerry who tried to handle situations the way Davidson did. After that, Jerry was on patrol alone and enjoying it. He was very busy and there was a lot of action. Jerry said he was busier than a cat in heat.

Jerry got a call from a man saying that someone was calling for help. He responded and when he got there the man met him and said he heard it but didn't know where it was coming from. Jerry stood there a minute then he heard it as well. He went behind the man's house and the call was louder there. His yard backed up to a church so Jerry walked that way and it got louder still. He walked around the church and still could not pin point where it was coming from. Finally he said "It seems to be coming from the top of the church." The caller went back and got a ladder and Jerry climbed up on the roof and heard the call again, coming from the chimney.

He walked over and shown his flashlight down the chimney. All he could see was black and two eyes looking up at him. "What's the purpose of your being down there? And, don't try to tell me you're cleaning the chimney." "I was going to steal the stereo equipment and got stuck," he half sobbed. Jerry said "Good enough for me, I'll see what I can do." He told the caller who was still below, what happened and the caller went back to his house and got a rope. Jerry tossed one end down the chimney and the guy was able to get it under his arms. With Jerry pulling up and he climbing it still took over twenty minutes to get him out. He was a 17 year old teen and he intended to get into the church then open the door for his 15 year old buddy to get in to steal the equipment. He was solid black from head to toe. Jerry said "Well, you may not have intended to clean the chimney but you did a good job." Jerry made the arrest and took him to jail in his car. It took half a day to get his car clean.

He started to work for Sergeant Phil, about six months later. Unfortunately the time Jerry spent with Fredrick and all the things Fredrick managed to screw up was what Sergeant Phil was basing his opinion of Jerry on.

It still took several months before he seemed to earn the Sergeant's respect. Phil was not riding his ass, so Jerry just strived to do the job the best that he could. After about three months, three of the veterans met him in the locker room and said "Hey, you don't have to be such a damn hot dog." Jerry answered, "I'm not trying to be a hot dog." "Well you sure as hell are being one." "No, I am not. I am just out there doing my job. No skin off your ass." "Yes it is. Your makin' us look bad." "If you're afraid of lookin' bad, I suggest you kick it up a notch or two." They walked away. A few weeks later Sergeant Phil called a squad meeting and read the previous month's stats. He said "One officer has done 9/10 of the work and what the hell were the rest of you doing? You better step it up or move out." The rest of the crew gave Jerry the cold shoulder, but did step it up and actually began to enjoy the feeling of doing well.

Jerry was on the department soft ball team and one afternoon, after the game, he and a fellow officer had stopped at a hardware store for a fitting he needed. The store was next to a bank and on the other side of the hardware store there was a bar. As Jerry and his friend where coming out of the hardware store they saw a man with a ski mask over his face come out of the bank and as he walked toward them he pulled his ski mask up. He then walked into the bar on the other side of the hardware store. Jerry and his friend were not sure if the man robbed the bank, but decided to do a little checking. Neither had a weapon so they just went into the bar and seeing the man ordering a beer at the bar, sat down on either side of him. Soon they heard sirens and saw police cars pull up to the bank. They watched through the bar

windows and could tell by the position the cars took that they were responding to a robbery call. They waited until the man put both his hands on the bar then each of them grabbed him putting an arm lock on him and marched him out on his tip toes and turned him over to the police. He had the bank money still on him.

Instead of getting an "Atta boy", they were reprimanded for not carrying guns at all times. While they were not to carry guns while participating in a sporting event they were required to carry them at all other times. Since they were on their way home they should have been armed.

One afternoon in early spring Jerry was on patrol during some heavy flooding, in north Bend near Snoqualmie, a man was moving a little too fast and lost control of his car right in front of Jerry. He went off the road and into the river. The man got out and waded through chest high water to the shore. The car was caught in the current and was slowly being sucked downstream. Jerry saw two little girls in the back seat. They were about three and five years old. Jerry leapt out of his car, threw off his gun belt and jumped into the river. He worked his way out to the car and was able to pull both girls out of the car just as the car was pulled into the current and away downstream and carried the girls to shore. The father just stood there on the shore and watched.

When the girls were safe Jerry called the fire department paramedics to check the girls out. The father mumbled a halfhearted thank you like someone might thank someone for holding a door for them. The man called his wife and as soon as she got there she started yelling at her husband and said nothing to Jerry or the paramedics. Once again, no "Atta boy."

One night about 11:00pm Jerry was on patrol driving down Interstate 90 in the Mercer tunnel. There was a black man in a Mustang who had run out of gas and was blocking a lane of traffic in the middle of the tunnel. Jerry stopped to help him but could see that there would be a few problems. The back of the car was jacked up so far that Jerry wouldn't be able to push him and because there was a slight grade it would be impossible to push him by hand. Jerry's unit had the same set of specs as the cars that the state patrol had. They were equipped with a fuel transfer pump that allowed them to pump gas to stalled vehicles that were out of gas, so that they did not have to carry a gas can around. It was a '74 Polaris with a 426 Hemi engine. Their department, however, issued an order that none of their officers were to use these pumps. They also had to sign a direct order not to use them.

Well, seeing no other way to help the man move his car, Jerry used it. He hooked it up, ran the hose to the man's car, examined it thoroughly with a flash light and when he was sure it was ok, turned the pump on. He went to the back of his car to direct traffic while it was running. It only took five minutes to pump two gallons, but before it had run two minutes he heard a loud "FROOOOOMPPP.!" He turned around and looked to see his entire car in flames. Evidentially there was a pin hole leak in the line and because of the incline fuel was running under his car. He ran up, opened the door turned off the motor and grabbed the keys which turned the pump off, then ran around, opened the trunk, grabbed the fire extinguisher and put the fire out.

Meanwhile the other man had run as far away as he could. When the fire was out he came back and thanked Jerry for helping him and drove off. A passerby had called the fire department and when they showed up they asked Jerry if he wanted them to call for a tow. Jerry said he wanted to see if it would start first and it did. The fire Chief followed him back to the county garage with his lights flashing and Jerry's car running on three cylinders all the way. He traded it for another car and went back to work. He was convinced he was going to get fired. A week later there was a large envelope in his box and he just knew he would be out of a job. WRONG. He actually received a commendation for bravery for putting the fire out. Nothing for saving two little girls but an award for putting a fire out that he started??? He never could understand the way the department worked.

*   *   *   *   *   *   *   *   *   *   *   *   *   *

One evening, just after dark, Jerry was dispatched to a rural home to a fight between a father and son. When he got there the father met him in the drive-way and said he and his son had been arguing about school. He said that his son had taken his 22 rifle and gone to the barn. He was afraid of what his son might do with the gun. Jerry called out to the barn and identified himself as a policeman then walked around the house toward the barn using his flash light to see the way. About 200 feet from the barn, he called again identifying himself. He heard a shot, but didn't see a muzzle flash. He wasn't sure what it was and didn't associate it with the gun shot. He thought he may have bumped a branch or something. He identified himself again then walked into the barn. The boy was about 14 years old and very distraught and upset.

He was standing there crying. The gun was leaning against a bale of hay and Jerry picked it up, unloaded it and asked what he planned on doing with it. The boy said "Nothin." Then Jerry asked him what he shot at. Again the boy answered, "Nothin." Jerry took him back to the house and the three of them went to the kitchen and sat down and were talking. Jerry was thinking that he was going to be able to slide easily out of this one. The Dad flopped down in a chair next to Jerry looking exhausted. He looked at Jerry, then pointed at him and said "Hey, you better check yourself." Jerry looked down at his jacket and saw a tiny little hole. He opened his jacket, looked at his shirt and saw a wet spot about the size of a dime. He was really surprised! He asked the kid, "What the hell did you shoot me for?" The boy sobbed, "I don't know."

Now Jerry was really embarrassed. He didn't want to put it out over the air, as they would make a big deal out of it. He called on the radio and asked if his Sergeant was near a phone. He was told he could reach Sergeant Phil on the precinct phone. Jerry called him and explained the circumstances. Jerry said "Don't get excited, it was no big deal, but it looks like I've been shot in the stomach with a 22." Phil asked what he wanted to do about it. Jerry said "Send another car to take care of the kid. I can't leave him here after shooting a cop. I can drive myself to the hospital." Phil got really pissed off, "You stupid fucking son of a bitch, you are in more trouble than that kid. You sit your ass down. I'll be there in a bit."

Meantime he sent an ambulance, another car and he showed up with a rookie in his car before the ambulance

48

got there. When he arrived he took all Jerry's gear and made him ride in the ambulance while the rookie drove Jerry's car back.

At the hospital Jerry was x-rayed and sent to surgery. They gave him some pain medication, then went in with forceps and took the bullet out. They gave him tetanus shot, put a Band-Aid on the wound and he went back to work. Boy did he get teased. They called him, Band-Aid boy for quite a while.

Shortly after that, Jerry heard Phil arguing with another Sergeant who wanted Jerry to work for him. Phil said "No way, I am not giving him up." Jerry felt he was finally reprieved.

*   *   *   *   *   *   *   *   *

Each precinct has several districts and each district has three shifts, day, swing and night. Jerry and his partner were working the second shift. They had good relations with the adjoining district.

One officer, Dan had two, four year college degrees and was working on his master's degree. However when it came to practical situations he was short on common sense.

A little girl was stolen from her front yard and everyone was looking for her. It was all over the news and all agencies were involved in the search for little Susie. The search had been going on for a week and every few hours there were updates on television, radio and in the newspapers. It happened in downtown Seattle. Jerry and his partner were working the east side that was a long way away from that area.

Dan was dispatched on a call from a citizen reporting what looked like a grave in the woods near a housing development. When he got there he saw a freshly dug plot of ground about the size of a child. There was a stick cross at the head. He called his Sergeant to report it. His Sergeant is reluctant, but doesn't want to take a chance and calls it into Homicide. It is Friday afternoon and

Homicide thinks patrol is trying to play a trick on them, so they tell patrol that if they, patrol, think it is important that they will need to guard it until morning as they have no one available at this time. Dan is sure this is the little girl and that someone should take care of it. Grave yard does not have enough people to guard it, so Jerry and his partner were assigned to guard it for the night.

At eight a.m. homicide shows up and digs it up. As they expected, it is some child's dog. Jerry and his partner are really pissed off. Not only did they lose a night sleep but won't get much rest before having to go back to work. They got back to the precinct at nine a.m. and turned their car in. They decide to get even with Dan. They know that he will still be sleeping, so they go into an interview room and called Dan on the phone. Jerry had a cloth over the phone to disguise his voice. He says, "Officer Jones?" Dan answers, "Yes, This is Sergeant mumble, mumble from homicide. We need you to come down to homicide immediately." Dan gets really excited and said "It was her, wasn't it? I knew it was. I knew it was." Jerry said "We can't discuss it over the phone, come down here immediately," and hangs up.

Their offices are in north King County and Criminal Investigation Division. CID, offices that house homicide are in downtown Seattle. It is twenty miles away.

Dan drives downtown goes into CID. However since it is the weekend, they are closed. There are benches in the hallway outside the door so he sits down and waits. He sits there for four hours. Now it is time for him to get back to work. He walks across the hall to the com-center and picks up the phone that goes to the com-center supervisor and asks when CID is going to get there? Com center asks, "Why the hell would they be coming in at all?" Dan said "Because I was told to come down here about the body." The super says, "What body?" "The one they dug up this morning." "Oh, you mean the dog?" Dan said "Will you please call them for me?" The super says, "No way will I call homicide on a weekend. Go back to your precinct." Dan went back and filled out an overtime slip for all the time he was down there and turns it in to his Sergeant. His Sergeant said "What the hell is this?" Dan explains. The Sergeant says, "You dumb son of a bitch, you've been had." He throws the slip away.

The next morning Jerry called again. "This is Sergeant "mumble, mumble" from homicide, sorry for the mix up. Resubmit your overtime and it will be covered," and hangs up before Dan can ask any questions. So, Dan did. You could hear his Sergeant throughout the whole precinct. "You dumb son of a bitch. How could anyone with your level of education be so fuckin' stupid?"

Whenever an officer goes on duty he draws a car at the start of a shift. It is always good to be one of the first ones there to get one you know is a good one. The officer then pulls it out of the parking spot, gets out and walks around it checking for any dents or scratches and logs them so that he won't get charged for them. He also needs to check the oil, water and gas as well as the shot gun to be sure it is loaded and that nothing is in the barrel. The previous night Dan had come in and parked his car with the passenger side right against the fence. The next officer to use the car pulls it out and does the walk around. To his surprise the whole passenger side is wiped out from the front fender all the way to the back. It is just crumbled. He reports it. The Sergeant called Dan and asks, "What the hell happened to the car?" Dan said "I don't know it was fine when I parked it there." The Sergeant asks Jerry if he has any idea and Jerry had a felling he might and said "I have something I want to check out and I'll let you know."

In the middle of Jerry's district is a large dairy farm. They would shovel manure into wagons and haul it across the highway to the hay fields and spread it on the ground. At that crossing was a curve that was always slippery when wet and it had rained the night before. Jerry drove out there to check. There was a telephone pole on the curve. Jerry got out and looked at it and sure enough there is white paint, chrome and part of the police insignia on the pole. Jerry talked to the farmer and he said that he had pulled Dan out of the ditch with his tractor. Jerry told the Sergeant and he called Dan back in hopes of hearing the truth. Dan lied again and was fired.

*   *   *   *   *   *   *   *   *   *   *   *   *   *

There were times when things happened that defied explanation. Jerry had responded to a burglary call and was at the woman's house making the report. It was 8:00pm and her phone rang. She answered it and said it was for Jerry. Dispatch was calling and wanted him to respond to a call about a 19 year kid, barricaded in a basement with a gun. The father of the kid was a sports store gun buyer and had a lot of guns in his basement. He said his son had, "flipped out" and they were afraid of him killing them. The house was nearby and Jerry was the closest officer available. The house was on a steep hill and Jerry parked about half way up the block under a street light. Another police car arrived and as Jerry got out he heard a shot. The other police car had his window down and heard it as well. Jerry ran alongside of the other car until they were clear. Then they ran around the front and down the side of the house so they could see inside. The blinds were closed and they couldn't see anything but heard the sound of someone pounding nails.

Just then Sergeant Phil pulled up and parked behind Jerry's car. Jerry yelled at him, "Don't park there. Don't park there." The Sergeant stood up and said "Huh?" Just then the kid leaned out the window and fired a shot at Phil. He started running up the hill as fast and low as he could. It was really comical as no part of his body was higher than 8" off the ground. Jerry stepped forward with his gun drawn to distract the kid, and said "HEY." He turned and looked at Jerry and ducked back inside and disappeared. About 30 feet in front of the big daylight basement window was a big landscaping boulder with a perfect view of the inside of the basement. Jerry was able to get behind that before the kid could see him.

Meanwhile Phil came down on the back side of the house and tried to negotiate with the kid. He had one of the only portable radios available at that time. He called the shift Lieutenant and told him to bring tear gas. When he got there he handed Phil a room sized gas cartage. Phil said "That's not big enough." He reached in to the supply box and pulled out a crowd control gas grenade. He went around the house and threw a rock in the window then yelled to the kid "You've got 30 seconds to come out or I will gas you." Jerry said "For Christ sakes, don't tell him what you are going to do he might just shoot you." Phil waited and got no response so he threw the grenade in and when he did the kid shot at him. It went off and in 30 seconds the kid bailed out the other window. Before he could get up Jerry was on him and had cuffed him. As he was reading him his rights the boy said he was a moon God and that he was under direct orders from the high supreme moon God leader. He had commanded him to kill his parents and everyone he could.

He was arrested and committed to an institution. The parents couldn't use their home for a long time. Even after three months, every time they turned the heater on the house would reek of tear gas.

About two years later before roll call one morning, Sergeant Phil looked up as Jerry was walking in. He said "Hey Jerry, I put your name on the Dick list." Jerry said "I don't think I am ready for that." "Oh yes you are. At your age you have to jump at every chance you get." "Ok, I'll take the test. Thanks I think."

*   *   *   *   *   *   *   *   *   *   *   *   *   *

It usually took five to seven years before a patrolman took the test to become a detective. Jerry had only worked a little over three years. He had a lot of studying to do. A month later he was taking the test. He got the second highest score. The officer that scored the highest was a real asshole but in spite of it was taken on as a detective. He didn't last long. He thoroughly screwed up his district and Jerry was transferred to take his place. This made him an instant enemy for the rest of Jerry's career even though Jerry never did anything to him.

It took Jerry 12 hours a day, 6 days a week to get everything caught up. A detective was assigned about 30 cases per month and was expected to close them all by the end of the month. They were not supposed to let cases roll over into the following month. That man had fifty-five cases active and twenty-five pending. Some were at least four or five months old. Some even had good leads that he hadn't followed. Jerry didn't know what the heck he had been doing, but he damn sure wasn't doing his job. What a mess. It took Jerry over 2 months to close all the open cases. Sergeant Schmidt was the head of larceny and property crimes. He was a no nonsense man, well-muscled, with piercing blue eyes. He was 6' 3" and bald as a baby. When he was really angry the whole top of his head turned beet red. Most of the men liked him as he was always fair. The precinct had an In and Out board and the men were to sign out whenever they left the building and put down their destination. Schmidt did not like that at all. He said that his detectives shouldn't have to be accountable for every second on the job. He told his men to just write in I.T.W. when they left. (In The Wind.).

The officers would watch Schmidt when he was reading a report and if his head turned red they just had to hope that it wasn't their report he was reading. The men knew they could not lie to him or falsify a report. They were convinced he was physic. He seemed to always be on top of everything that went on.

Jerry's friend, Bart, who made detective the same time Jerry did, was in the same situation. He also had replaced someone who had left a mess, in an adjoining district.

They would always back each other up. Bart was 5'9", very muscular had a heavy mustache, was bald on

54

top with brown, monk-styled hair around the sides. His eyes were always sparkling with intelligent good humor and he knew how to make a good joke out of any situation. His mother worked at a well-known waterfront sea food restaurant. The two friends would go there about once a month and she would treat them especially well. One afternoon they decided to sneak out and go there on their lunch break. When they signed out, with the customary I.T.W. Schmidt saw them leaving and called over to them, "Hey, be sure and try the shrimp, it is really great." "How the heck did he know where we were going?" asked Bart "I told you he was physic," Jerry shot back.

Jerry and Bart were working Saturdays and extra hours, trying to clean up all the old cases their predecessors left. Schmidt had informed them that there was no authorized paid overtime or compensation but they did it on their own. They thought that Schmidt didn't know about it. One day Schmidt called them into his office, (when they were almost caught up) and said "If you boys can't do this job in eight hours, I'll find someone who can." They realized that it was his way of telling them to slow down.

Jerry had the Eastern part of the county. It was mostly rural and there were a lot of farms, logging operations and construction jobs going on. One day Jerry was assigned a case from a logging company saying that a lot of equipment had been stolen. Jerry responded and drove to a logging project closest to the company that had experienced the theft. He drove up, got out of the car and was interviewing some of the men there when some ass hole came up and started yelling at him, calling him names, berating police in general and getting in his face.

The man was 6' 4" and 260 lbs. He came forward and shoved Jerry hard, in the chest. The fight was on. Jerry was afraid the other men would come after him as well. He was there to help them, and he didn't under-stand what this guy's problem was. The man kept at him,

mostly wrestling but throwing a few punches as well. He was punching Jerry and kicking him with his steel-toed work boots.

He was doing a good job of tearing Jerry's suit up and this really pissed Jerry off. This was money out of Jerry's pocket. Jerry lit into him and got him face down in a ditch. There was a piece of dirty rope there so he grabbed it and hog tied the ass hole. Jerry tied the guy's hands behind his back and his feet to his hands so he couldn't kick him anymore. Then Jerry had an inspiration. He dragged the guy to the car opened the trunk, took out his evidence kit and put it in the back seat and then he threw the guy in. Jerry was really pissed off now, his whole suit was torn up. The guy continued to yell and cuss at him,

"You untie me you son of a bitch and I'll kick your fuckin' ass all over this place." Jerry got in the car and drove off. None of the other men said a word, they just watched with surprised looks on their faces.

When Jerry got down to the main line, about a mile away, he took the next spur road. He knew it went twelve miles to the site where the theft took place. He knew no one would be there this late in the day. When he got there he dragged the guy out of the trunk and untied him. By now the guy was pretty humble and apologetic. Jerry reasoned that he probably thought that Jerry took him way up there to shoot him.

He told Jerry how two guys came to their site to try and sell a bunch of equipment, but they didn't want it because they were pretty sure it was stolen. He said they had all kinds of stuff, just about anything that they could have carried away from a site. Probably about $6,000 to $7,000 worth. He gave a good description of the two men and the name of a gal they were supposedly staying with. He also told Jerry about the bar where they hung out. Jerry got in the car and turned on the motor. He said "You need to take some time to think about what an asshole you've been." then drove off. He heard later that the man didn't get back to the main line until about 1:00am, when the security guard found him walking and picked him up.

The next day, Jerry was able to make the arrest and get most of the equipment back. Both of the men had felony warrants out on them, from California. They were more than happy to come after them.

This really established Jerry's reputation. The story was all over the area by the next day He now had the respect and cooperation from everyone, including fellow officers. He was amazed at how fast word spread. He hadn't told anyone, yet everyone seemed to know about it. The editor of the local paper who was a friend of his called him and wanted the story. Jerry just told him it was blown out of proportion and wouldn't say any more. He didn't want to look like a glory hound.

*   *   *   *   *   *   *   *   *   *   *   *   *

Chapter 3
A Detective's Work is Never Done

Evidently Jerry's efforts to let the public know that they needed more police to take care of all their needs, paid off. Some of those folks that he offered the fifty-seven cents to must have raised cane. First the county was awarded a federal grant to hire and outfit 104 new officers. Then, it became a requirement that all police had to be academy trained. The grant would also cover the new officer's first year salary.

Every department scrambled to have their own academy. They had to staff it, establish a curriculum, obtain a location, and get it up and running. One hell of a lot of work and man power. To make it work they had to pull police off the street. This of course resulted in a shortage of police available to work the streets. It also created a lot of animosity. Everyone was working with a lot less and thought that everyone else was doing less work than they were.

Each department started hiring like crazy, going over the list of eligible people, who had passed the tests but were not hired as there was no available job at the time they passed, Unfortunately a lot of these people had gone on to get other jobs when they weren't hired.

In the past paid overtime was almost impossible to get. Now the officers could work themselves to death. A lot of the street officers were working back to back ten hour shifts.

One newsman happened to see an officer asleep in his car and took a photo of him. He printed it in the paper. There was no mention of the fact that the officer was off duty or that he had just finished an eighteen hour shift. -

After the first class of rookies graduated from the academy they were sent out into the field. Jerry and his fellow officers had never been to an academy as it was not in existence in the past. They did however have a lot of

58

hard years in the field.   It became the veteran's responsibility to provide field training for the rookies.

In the Field Training Officer program, Recruits ride with experienced officer for eight weeks.   Every day the recruit will sit down with the officer he rode with and be evaluated. They discussed how he did and what he needed to improve or do differently.   Once a week the two of them would meet with the Sergeant in his office to discuss where the recruit was in the program.

To begin with they were asked to take the rookies out but it soon became a requirement. They would put the rookies with different veterans each day to learn different techniques.   The veterans were not paid any extra and often had to work overtime with no extra pay. Needless to say enthusiasm was at an all-time low for both veterans and rookies. It was really hard when rookies made dumb mistakes. Then a veteran was forced to work with them to correct it and they were extra hard on the rookie.

Peet was a senior officer that had flat refused to take a rookie until his boss made it an order.   Peet was extremely intelligent, jaded and crusty. He was 5' 10" and took no shit off anyone. He didn't care who you were, you didn't mess with him.   He didn't go looking for trouble, but in an emergency you could count on Peet to handle it right. He was a good cop and knew it.

Finally, one dark stormy night, when it was raining hard he was ordered to take a rookie out.   About half way through his shift his Sergeant called him to meet at his car. The Sergeant didn't utterly trust Peet to treat the kid right.   When Peet got there the rookie wasn't with him. The Sergeant said "Where the hells your rookie?" Peet said "Guarding the 7-11." "Why is he guarding the 7-11?"   "In case it gets robbed."   "Do you have any information that it's going to be robbed?" "No, but it gets robbed all the time."   "Where did you leave him in the store?" "He's not in the store." "Peet, where the hell did you leave him?" the Sergeant fumed. "In the woods." "In the woods." "Why the hell did you leave him in the woods." "So he could keep an eye on the 7-11." The Sergeant was really pissed now. "Let's go get him. Right now!" They went to the woods, across from the 7-11 and got him. He was soaked and shivering but they had to give him credit, he had stuck to his post.

The Sergeant took the rookie back to the precinct, warmed him up and gave him to someone else.

Jerry gets a new rookie, Bill. Standard procedure has the rookie ride along for three days. They handle the details while the officer observes them. On the second half of the third day they get to drive the patrol car. It was seven p.m. Bill was driving and they were approaching a 711 store. They always pull into the parking area and drive through slowly as the 711 stores are often robbed. They were just coming in and a guy comes running out, jumps into his car and takes off. The store clerk comes running out waving at the police car, yelling and pointing at the fleeing car. The officers cannot hear what he is yelling but Jerry tells Bill to go after him. The car heads up the road and makes a left turn. They come roaring up behind him and Jerry is braced for a left turn when the Bill turns right. Jerry yells, "What the fuck are you doing?" Bill said "Well, the sign says no left turn." Jerry said "Pull over and stop." Jerry gets out, walks around the car, holds his finger up to keep him quiet and to try and calm down before carefully trying to explain that as a cop, they may need to violate a traffic law in order to expedite catching a bad guy. Jerry said "Didn't you notice that the other guy made a left turn there?" "Yea." "Well, what did you think?" "I don't know." Jerry said "You are never allowed to say that for the next 19.9 years. That is unacceptable." "What should I say?" "You can say, I thought this or that, I wasn't aware or I will study to find out. I don't know, is what a two year old says to his mother." As it turned out the man had stolen some candy. Bill turned out to be an excellent officer.

Jerry's next rookie, Dusty was 6' tall, solid, intelligent, but not aggressive. He was so polite and soft spoken that Jerry was concerned that he might not be able to handle a bad situation. After about a week and a half they got a call about a man making a disturbance at a Safeway store. When they arrived the man was outside in a phone booth. He had slapped a Safeway employee and needed to be detained. Jerry told Dusty to handle it. Jerry watched as Dusty went to the booth and told the man to step out. The guy had wedged himself in with his arms. He said to Dusty, "Fuck You." Dusty reached in to pull him out and he slapped Dusty's hands away. Jerry can't see Dusty's face so is not sure how he is going to handle it. He reaches in again and this time the guy spits in his face. Dusty grabs him and forcibly snatched him out of the booth then face prints him and cuffs him. Jerry thinks, "Way to go Dusty." He turned out to be a really great officer.

The next recruit that is assigned to Jerry was Tyrone. He was six feet six, black, tall and skinny and not too overly bright. When Jerry asked about his past he found that when Tyrone was younger he did drugs and even dealt. On Tyrone's third day, Jerry did a fire arms inspection. It was all wrong. His gun was empty. Jerry asked, "Did you just unload your gun?" He said "No." Jerry asked, "Well why isn't it loaded?" Tyrone answered, "No one told me I could load it." Jerry was amazed, "You mean you have been on patrol driving around in a marked police car, in full uniform with an empty gun?" "Yea." Jerry could not get through to him how dumb that was, in a nice way.

The next morning Tyrone shows up for roll call and his pants are up around his knees. Jerry thought someone pulled a trick on him. Everyone knew how to pick a locker so Jerry thought someone had changed pants with him. The pants were 100% wool and $300 a pair. If they were worn out or damaged in the line of duty you could get another pair. Tyrone said "No they are my pants." Jerry said "What the hell happened?" "I took them home and washed them and put them in the dryer." Jerry thought Tyrone was shitin' him, no one could be that dumb. "No really, what happened?" Tyrone said "Really, I washed them and put them in the dryer and this is what happened." After roll call Jerry and Tyrone went into the Sergeant's office and had an hour and a half talk. Tyrone quit.

Jerry went in and talked to his boss. He was bitching about training recruits. He said that here he hadn't even been to the academy and he was training recruits that had been through it. It didn't make a whole lot of sense. His boss said " Tough shit, no one else that is doing 'the on the job training' has been either." Then he issued Jerry another rookie.

Rick was competent right off the bat. Jerry and Rick had a special chemistry and couldn't turn around without running into something major. They worked so well together that they became the talk of the precinct.

They went to a house on a loud music complaint. They were in full uniform and they knocked on the door. A man answered opened the door and without even looking at them said "About God damn time you got here." Then he turned around and led them into the front room. There were six guys sitting in a circle on the rug with three kilos of marijuana in front of them. Jerry said in a loud and friendly voice, "Hi guys." They all looked up and almost shit. Rick and Jerry arrested them all and called the "jail van" to come and haul them in. They confiscated the drugs as well.

A couple of nights later they were driving around and they went by a man who had the back of a camper open and was taking a large tool box out. He had it on the tail gate and was about ready to take it off. Usually cops would drive on by thinking it was the owner but they stopped and said "What are you doing?" The guy sees them and takes off running. He didn't get five steps when Rick had him. They contacted the house and the owner was very thankful. He said that the box was full of specialty auto tools worth over $10,000.00. The camper had been locked. They were able to charge 'the would be thief' with grand theft as he had taken the box out of the camper.

On another night they were driving down a road in a heavily populated residential area. As they drove by a side street and looked down they saw a tail light flash about three fourths of a block down the street. They backed up and turned down that street. There were a lot of cars parked along the street and Rick opened the door as they drove slowly along and stood looking down into cars as they went by. They were showing their light into the parked cars. About four or five cars down they spotted a kid laying on the floor boards and a stereo about half out of the dash. They arrested him then contacted the house and they were very happy that their equipment was not taken.

*　*　*　*　*　*　*　*　*　*　*　*　*　*

As enough officers became available to take their places the senior officers had to take the sixteen week course at the academy. Jerry was pissed off because he got stuck with all the senior officers. They had lived through everything the instructors were trying to shove down their throat and resented having to listen to someone who had never been there and done that. All of them except Jerry had over twice the time in the field as their instructors. It made it really hard for the instructors to teach them anything. They actually ran one of the instructors out of the classroom.

Jerry had attended with the hope of learning what he could and he felt sorry for the instructors. The old timers would argue with everything they said at the drop of a hat.

He felt that he would have learned more in a different group. In spite of all the arguing and discontent, he did feel that he got a lot of good information and enjoyed the experience.

After graduation he was certified as a police officer of the state of Washington. This met that he did not have to worry about jurisdiction and could work anywhere in the state.

*　*　*　*　*　*　*　*　*　*　*　*　*　*

Jerry spent the next two years working burglary and larceny. The following six months working robbery. The next six months he spent working homicide.

He was then assigned to the Undercover Criminal Investigating Unit, (UCI). He had only worked in the department a short time when homicide came to his Sergeant and asked if Jerry and his partner could work a case for them. Homicide was slammed and needed help. Jerry's Sergeant wanted Jerry to take the new kid with him as he felt it would be a good chance for him to learn investigating procedures and the specialized paperwork that had to be done. When presenting a case to court the written report had to be in a certain format. The new kid had no experience and could learn a lot. Therefore Jerry and his Sergeant agreed to take the cases for homicide. Ted was a good kid. 5'9" about 160 pounds, average build with dark hair and a laid back attitude. Almost spacy. He had a good sense of humor and was quick with the come-backs. He had a college degree and was no dummy. He was a definite "follower" though. He always said "As long as I don't let go of your coat tails we'll have a hell of a run."

Jerry and Ted got the paperwork on the "Cadwell" case. Nancy Cadwell, a 13 year old babysitter, was sent home at midnight, about 4 blocks away, in a very small town and never got home. Parents had called to report her missing but the police could do nothing for 24 hours. Kids that age were prime run-away cases. Or, they would stop at a friend's and fall asleep watching T.V., or meet some other kids and sit around talking and forget the time.

When the girl had not returned by breakfast, the father had gone out looking for her. He had walked all around the small town. On his way back home, he was walking on the dike along the river. He looked out at the gravel bar and saw what he thought was clothing. He waded out and found his daughter's body, her pants and panties gone. The father pulled her body to shore and asked a passer-by to call the police. The police that responded, photographed the body and the scene, gathered evidence, then contacted the medical examiner who took control of the body. The medical examiner called homicide, but they were already out on other cases then asked patrol to take statements from the girl's family and the folks she had been babysitting for. Nancy's mother knew what she had been wearing and described all her clothing including her cream colored panties with small red hearts on them. Patrol sent the report and Jerry and Ted got it on Monday morning.

It took Jerry and Ted over an hour to read the findings then they changed into suits and drove to the small town. It was about forty miles out in the country. They talked to the girl's parents and the folks the girl had been babysitting for. Next they started interviewing the kids in town. It was summer so there was no school but they saw several kids in the city park. They were wearing their badges which identified them and talked to the kids. They learned that the girl was friendly and well liked. She was big breasted for a 13 year old and had no boyfriends. Soon there were 20 or 30 kids there. Almost too many to work with. The kids had a hard time believing they were detectives as both men had been doing undercover work and had beards and they drove a Trans-Am. Ted talked to the main group and Jerry took individuals aside if one seemed to have more to say. He could tell that a 17 year old boy in particular wanted to tell him something but was holding back. Jerry asked him to sit in the car, and began talking to him. He said "Withholding information on a homicide is a felony. You are old enough to be considered an adult and would go to prison. Believe me when I tell you that young white boys are raped in prison. I don't think you would enjoy that."

That was all it took. The boy started telling him about an 18 year old, who had been hanging out with them at their car club. Every time the deceased would walk by, Rick Chatman would make sexual comments to the guys. Things like, "I'd like to play with those titties." And "I would really like to screw that." Then he went on to say that he never saw Rick approach her or talk to her. Jerry asked if anyone else made any comments. The boy said "No, she was jail bait." The boy also told Jerry where Rick lived.

Jerry and Ted talked to several other kids as well for the next couple of hours then went to get something to eat and discussed the case. They decided to go talk to the Chatman boy.   He lived about a mile out of town on a small ranch.   The house was down a long driveway wide enough for three or four cars to park in front. The other boy said the Rick had a light blue Chevy. It was parked in front of the house. It was a three bedroom ranch house.

They got out of the car and as they walked by Rick's car, Jerry looked inside, then stopped and looked a little closer.   Ted said "What are you looking at?" Jerry said "Anything I can see." The girl had been stabbed in the neck, so there should have been a lot of blood. Jerry saw something sticking out of the crack in the back seat, a rag or something. He looked closer and saw a patch of cream color with little red hearts. He asked Ted if he knew how to write a search warrant. "No".

Jerry wrote the critical information on a paper and told Ted to get to a phone, call the prosecutors and tell him all the facts and that you are coming to town to get a warrant. Tell him it was for a homicide and time was critical. He also told him to be assertive as they would try to brush him off as they were busy too. He further told Ted that if they gave him any trouble to get hold of their Sergeant to put pressure on the prosecutor. He told Ted to wait until he made the arrest.

Then Jerry and Ted knocked on the door. Rick answered. He was a small kid, about 5'7" maybe 140 pounds. He was wiry, thin faced with intense eyes and scared. Jerry identified them and asked if his parents were home. No, they were both at work. Jerry asked him to step out of the house. He did. Jerry pointed to the blue car and asked if it was his. He said "Yes." Jerry had him line up against the wall and shook him down. He had a wallet, car keys, change, cash and a pocket knife. Jerry told Rick he was going to handcuff him for his protection and his. Then Jerry advised him of his rights and asked for consent to search his car. Rick agreed and Jerry took the handcuffs off and had him sign a consent form. Ted said "Why the hell do we need the warrant. We have a signed consent to search?" Jerry answered, "Because an attorney might get the consent to search thrown out of court, but couldn't get both kicked out." Ted then left to get the warrant.

Jerry re-cuffed Rick took him to their car and belted him into the front seat. He asked the kid if he was trained in any type of martial arts. "No." "Ok, if you promise me you won't give my any shit, I will handcuff you in front. But, if you try anything it will get ugly quick." Jerry explained. "I am detective Jorgenson, King Co. Police department. I am here investigating a homicide case. I'll bet you know why you're in hand-cuffs?" The kid was crying now, he said "Yes sir." Jerry went on, "Would you like to tell me about it?" Rick said "Yes sir." Jerry got the tape recorder out of his brief case, taped the basic intro, played it back to be sure the recorder was working right and said "This is detective Jorgensen, King Co. police department, badge number 8240. Today is June 7th, 1977. It is 3:45pm. We are located in the drive-way of the Chatman's home, sitting in the police vehicle, with Richard Chatman who has been placed under arrest and advised of his rights. - -

He stopped the recording, played it back to be sure he got it all and then went on. "This is detective Jorgensen talking to Rick Chatman, with his permission. Is that right Mr. Chatman?" Rick said "Yes sir." Jerry said "I have previously advised you of your rights and you understand them. Is that right Mr. Chatman?" "Yes sir." "As you fully understand these rights are you now willing to talk to me?" "Yes sir." "You already know what this is all about? Would you like to tell me about it?" Rick was crying "I really didn't mean to do it." Jerry said "Go on." The boy said "I was driving around town with nothing to do and I saw Nancy walking down the street. I pulled over and started talking to her. We were having a good time talking.

We were laughing a lot and I asked her if I could give her a ride home. She said Sure, and got in the car. I started driving toward her house then told her I wanted to show her something and drove up on the dike. It was only about 200 yards from her house. I parked the car and tried to kiss her. She said no and pushed me away. We started fighting and wound up in the back seat. Somehow her bra came undone and I grabbed her breast. She started screaming. I told her to shut up but she just kept screaming. I pulled out my knife, just to scare her and held it against her neck and told her to stop screaming.

She kept struggling and all of a sudden there was a sighing sound, like the air going out of a balloon. All the air went out of her and she just lay there. I thought she just gave up. I took her pants and panties off to screw

68

her. Then I realized she wasn't breathing. I checked her pulse and she didn't have any. I got really scared. I drug her out of the car and down the bank and into the river. I threw her pants in the river and went home. I got home, checked the car and didn't see anything, then came in and went to bed."

After Rick was through talking, Jerry called patrol to come and pick him up and transport Rick downtown. While he was waiting he filled out the booking sheet and charged Rick with Murder 1. He knew they could always plead down.

Jerry had to wait about an hour before Ted got back with the warrant. In the meantime the boy's mother got home from work. Jerry explained what had happened. Her son was under arrest for murder and his car and room were considered a crime scene and she was not to enter either one. He asked her to wait outside. She was very upset but was cooperating. Then she said that she was going to the neighbors and gave Jerry their phone number. She wanted a lot more information than Jerry could give her. He told her he would call and tell her everything as soon as possible. In those days there was no C.S.I. (Crime Scene Investigation unit), so when Ted got back, with the warrant, they took a dozen or so photos, took the panties, searched the bedroom, took a whole bag of Rick's dirty clothes, (they had no idea what he had been wearing) and impounded his car. They found no other weapons, no blood on his sheets or towel, they then secured the crime scene. Everything would be turned in as evidence. Ricks mother had called his Father and he arrived while they were searching the bedroom. "You can't keep me out of my own house." he boomed. Jerry answered, "Yes sir, right now I can. This isn't a house right now it is a crime scene. As soon as we are done here it will again become your house. I promise you that when we are done here I will come over and explain to you and your wife everything that is going on."

Jerry and Ted finished bagging everything about 11:00 pm. They had a whole car full of evidence. Then they drove to the neighbor's house, went in and gratefully accepted a cup of coffee. They sat down and Jerry said "I am truly sorry, but there is no easy or gentle was to tell you what happened. I will just tell you the facts. A young girl was killed last night and our investigation led to your son. He was very remorseful but has admitted to killing her. Your son had been very cooperative and the matter is now in the hands of the court." They asked if they should get an attorney. Jerry said that it would be a very good idea. He and Ted then left.

They took everything downtown to evidence for evaluation and what was workable to the crime scene lab. The knife was 3" long with a 2 ¼"blade that was 3/8" wide. When the boy held it to her neck, whether he pushed it or she surged against it was not clear, but in any case it entered her neck between two vertebrae's and severed her spine. Death was instantaneous. There was hardly any blood at all, only a trace on the knife. No major blood vessels were hit.

Jerry presented the case to the prosecutor after filling out 30 hours of paperwork that included the charge sheet. There was enough to fill a three ring binder about 2 ½" to 3" thick. Then he had to take it upstairs, take a number and wait until his number was called before he could present it. After the prosecutor read it he did not see that anything had to be done. About four or five days later however, Jerry got a call from the prosecutor who got the case. He wanted Jerry to take the panties out to the victim's mother for identification. Jerry said "That's bull shit. She has suffered enough. She can identify them just as easily in court." Then he hung up on the prosecutor. "Well", Jerry said "Shit rolls down hill and that turd came back to me real soon." The prosecutor called the homicide Sergeant, who called Jerry's Sergeant, who had unkind words to say to Jerry. Jerry went up, got the panties and tried to get Ted to do it. Ted said "Oh no, you're the lead detective on this case."

Jerry had to take them out to meet the mother. She met him in her kitchen and offered him a cup of coffee. He said "I am really sorry to have to do this. It is terribly uncomfortable for both of us and I really dislike it. I am afraid that I need to have you identify some- thing." He showed her the panties. "OH MY GOD! YES THOSE ARE HERS!" Then she broke down into heart rending spasms of tears. Then her husband came in and was furious. He yelled at Jerry to get out and blamed him for the message he brought. Jerry had to explain that if they wanted their daughter's killer prosecuted that he had to do it. he said "This is very unpleasant for me as well and I am so sorry but I had to do it." He got the signed statement and took it back to the prosecutor.

This case never went to trial as the suspect pleaded guilty all down the line. He pleaded to murder 2, meaning that it was not pre-meditated, and was sentenced to prison.

Strangely enough, a month or so after her son was convicted Jerry got a message that he had a female visitor at the front desk. Jerry was working undercover at the time and could not see any visitors. He asked the desk to take a message. It was Rick's mother. She brought Jerry a loaf of homemade bread and left a note. "Thank you for your kindness and consideration." At first Jerry thought it might be poisoned. The crew just threw it out. The bread looked really good. It had nuts, berries and raisins in it. The woman started bringing one once a week. The crew decided to feed the bread to John's horses. He didn't like his wife's horses and wanted to get rid of them. However the horses loved the bread and didn't get sick. After a month the crew decided that bread was ok. Then the minute the woman brought the bread in, someone would run to the store and get a pound of butter and the crew would eat it right there. The woman brought a loaf in once a week for about a year. Finally it tapered off. Jerry could never understand this. His psychiatrist friend thought it was a way to apologize for her son or somehow make amends.

* * * * * * * * * * * * * *

No sooner was that case finished than homicide dumped another case in their laps. This started as a bar fight, moved outside where it became a knife fight then one man drew a gun and shot the other. Jerry and Ted had to interview witnesses and do all the paperwork. Jerry hated homicide as the paperwork took between 30 to 100 hours.

They had set up an interview with a group of transvestites and Jerry was positive that he told Ted that they were transvestites. This was a very tough section of town and the only time they were available was about seven p.m. on a Friday night.

Jerry and Ted went to meet them. These men were all dressed up ready to go out. They were dressed like single woman would dress who was on the prowl. They looked very sexy and oozed sex appeal. The main witness was sitting at a kitchen table with Jerry giving his statement. Jerry's back was to Ted, when the one he was interviewing poked him and motioned with his/her head that he should look around. Jerry looked back and saw that the blond man who looked like a very sexy woman was hitting on Ted. Ted was flirting back. It was all

72

Jerry and the guy he was interviewing could do to keep from laughing out loud. This went on for about 20 minutes. All of a sudden Ted got a strange look on his face, his jaw fell down then he jumped up and ran out of the room. Everyone cracked up laughing.

Jerry finished and went out. Ted was out in the car. Jerry started to say something and Ted hollered, "Shut up, fuck you, you son of a bitch, don't talk to me." After that, every time Jerry tried to explain that he had told him they were transvestites, Ted said "Fuck you, you dirty son of a bitch, don't even talk to me." It didn't help any that somehow it got around the bull pen and the guys started teasing Ted. Some would put a doily on their heads and make kissie, kissie sounds at him. Once Jerry tried to press the matter and kept on Ted about it. A little later he had to stop the car and mail a letter. Jerry got out to mail it and Ted drove off and left him and didn't come back. Jerry had to take a bus back to the office. Ted was waiting there but Jerry didn't say anything. From them on he decided to leave it alone.

* * * * * * * * * * * * * *

To work undercover the unit had to be exceptional at moving surveillance. When other units needed someone followed, they would call Jerry's unit. At first they would take instructions from the other units, but soon learned to follow their own instincts.

The action that prompted this was when Jerry and Ted were asked to do moving surveillance on a guy who was supposed to do an armed robbery on a drug store. They knew he was planning a robbery. They did not know where and could do nothing until he did it. Jerry and Ted were following him and the wheel man with him. They followed them for four or five hours. They would go slow by a drug store, scope it out then leave.

Finally they came to a pharmacy and the robber jumped out and rushed in. The other man stayed in the car then parked it about 400' away at the end of the small

mall building. Ted had forgotten his vest so Jerry took his apart and gave one side of it to Ted. This gave both of them protection in front at least.

Jerry and Ted parked their undercover car on the other side of a motor home that was parked two spaces down from the drug store that was being hit. Jerry got his badge out and told the people in the area to move away. There was a woman with three kids and she would not leave. She wanted to see what would happen.

A whole lot was going on in a very short period of time. The plan called for Jerry to come out from behind the motor home as though he was just coming out of it. As the suspect was coming out of the drug store and approaching Jerry, he would cold cock him as he walked past. Other units would be responsible for the suspect still in the car. Another unit was about 75' away to the north of the drug store. In those days there were no portable radios, so once things were in motion there was no communication and no way to share the plan.

As the suspect came out of the store and started walking south toward Jerry, one of the officers at the north end yelled, "STOP, police, you are surrounded." Jerry saw a big blue ball of flame in front of the suspect and knew he had been fired upon. He immediately fired at the suspect but knew he missed because his badge case was in the way. He dropped his badge case and immediately fired a second shot and saw a puff of smoke on the man's chest. He didn't go down. Jerry thought, "Shit, he has a vest on." He hadn't felt the recoil from his shot and thought that the property room and armory man had given him some bad ammo. Jerry aimed at the suspects balls and fired another round. The suspect spun and went down. Meanwhile, other shots were being fired. Jerry went running up to him and as he approached, the suspect was reaching behind him. Jerry grabbed his arm and cuffed him. The SOB was reaching for his second gun.

When the medics got there they were going to cut his pants off. Jerry, who also had medical training, told them not to. The man was so skinny, that his tight pants were the only thing that was keeping him from bleeding out from the wound. After the shooting stopped, some of the people in the near-by bar came out and told them several bullets had hit inside the bar and just missed one of them.

Everyone swooped in. They took Jerry's gun and sent him back to the precinct to fill out reports. Jerry felt like a criminal. He knew it was coming but still made him feel like he had done something wrong.

When Jerry got back to the precinct he called the hospital to see how the suspect was doing. The hospital said that he had lost too much blood and died. Jerry had to fill out three hours of paper work. Then, about four hours later his Sergeant came in and said "You know that guy you shot? Looks like he is going to make it." Jerry had to make all the paper work out again. That reminded him again about how much he hated homicide.

After six months in the unit he spent three months investigating mafia activity in the area. The San Francisco police had informed them that the #2 east coast mafia Don had been in San Francisco, gone into business under another name, then killed his business partner. It seems he and his family were under protective custody as he had made a deal with the U.S. Attorney to testify against the east coast mob. When the U.S. Marshal found out that the San Francisco police were investigating the murder of the business partner they swooped the family up and moved them. The police had an informant that said they were relocated to the Seattle area. They advised against letting the Marshal's office know that they were aware of this.

Homicide called Jerry's Sergeant and told him what they needed. They wanted Jerry and Ted to assist as they needed someone who was used to undercover work. The Sergeant okayed the request. When Jerry found out about it he said "Don't be so fuckin' helpful. You might at least talk to us first."

Jerry and Ted found the Don's new address by going through the business license office. He had started a new business, right away, under a different name. It was, however, the only new business license applied for in the last month and they knew what business he would be in.

They parked their van nearby and waited for someone to come out. They had three state of the art, auto advance cameras and would take as many photos as possible. Jerry said "You know how the mob members are always depicted as big burley guys? Well, they are." Jerry's driver parked the van and then walked away and left him. He didn't say a word. Jerry had no idea where he went. The Don and his two lieutenants walked out to the limo. Jerry was taking photos like crazy and had already used two cameras. Suddenly the Don pointed toward the van and said "Whose van is that?" They answered "I don't know." "Well, go find out." UH, OH!! If Jerry's driver didn't lock the van, he was in BIG TROUBLE. If they found out he was a cop, he was dead.

He quickly thought, I will tell them I am a news man. Maybe then they will only break my legs and smash my camera. It was a pretty scary moment. The muscle tried the front door and it was locked. Then he came around to the back. Jerry was ready to spring out and hit them as hard as he could and run. Thank God the back was locked too. One of them tried to look into the curtained window and said out loud, "I think I see someone in there." Jerry thought, Oh fuck here it comes. Just then, Jerry's driver came strutting up, unlocked the van got in and started it up. The mobster said "What the fuck are you doing here?" He shot back "I'm doing driveway appraisals." and drove off.

After the photos were developed they sent copies to San Francisco and the men were identified as the Don and his lieutenants. Then Jerry and Ted took a position on the hill above, so they could kept track of the family.

A short time later, Antonio, the Don's son moved out on his own, as he was a heavy drug user and the family did not allow the use of drugs. Antonio was having a party for his doper friends at his new home and was bragging about his connections to the mob. A biker guest said something derogatory to him then turned around to repeat it to his buddy. While his back was turned Antonio stuck a .44 under the bikers chin and blew his brains out. Witnesses said it launched him clear to the ceiling. The biker fell on the carpet. The son and another man just cut a big square out of the carpet, rolled the biker up in it and threw him in their van. Then they dumped him in the river. The son didn't bother to clean anything up. He was using pretty heavily and was loaded, wasted. Several of the other party guests decided to get out while they could.

The killing was witnessed by several people at the party. Antonio was so arrogant that he felt he could do anything to anybody and get away with it under the witness protection program.

Homicide found out where Antonio lived and knew that the killing had taken place there. They also heard that the man had a gun in every corner of the house and was trained in every type of martial arts. He repeatedly boasted that he wouldn't be arrested without a major fire fight.

Homicide wanted Jerry and Ted to go undercover as construction workers on the house that was being built across the street. They had contacted the contractor and told him that they needed to put two men on the job, undercover, to observe for the day. He had agreed to work Jerry and Ted into the project. Antonio's car was parked at the curb in front of his house, about 50' away. The goal was to watch him and when he came outside, take him down with the most expedient means possible. They were not to approach the house or put themselves in a position that would allow Antonio to re-enter the house. Hopefully, this would be the time he would have access to fewer weapons.

Jerry and Ted thought this was a bad idea. Homicide really had no idea how dopers operated. They might party for days. The construction crew would not be working at night so there would be no coverage, should Antonio choose to leave then.

Dopers often slept until noon or later and did most of their business at night.

Jerry and Ted had an old beat up van and their assigned radio man Earl was in the back with his equipment. He was in touch with homicide units who were in position in a three block radius around Antonio's house. They were parked about a quarter mile away waiting for the word that all other units were ready. Ted said "We aren't going to follow their plan are we?" Jerry answered, "We followed it last time and look what happened. We had to wind up shooting the guy and put a lot of civilians in danger." Earl piped up "Look guys, I am in this van too! Don't go getting my ass in trouble." "Oh Earl, come on, would we do that to you?" Earl leaned back and said "Ahhhh shit!" Then they got the call to go in.

Ted said "What are we gonna do?" "I don't know, we haven't seen the lay-out yet, we'll make it up when we get there." Earl kept saying "Ahh shit! Ahh shit!" over and over. They turned the corner approaching the house and there was Antonio's Trans Am, his pride and joy, all gussied up right on the street curb. As they drove up, Jerry barked the brakes skidding the tires just enough to leave a skid mark. It sent Earl tumbling and swearing. Then they pulled into the driveway of the house under construction. They got out of the van and walked to the house and went inside hoping Antonio would come out to check his car. No luck. Although they saw a window shade move no one came out. Ted and Jerry looked at each other and Jerry said "We can't let this get old. Let's go." Ted said "What are we doing?" "Just follow me." They walked toward Antonio's house and as they passed the van, Earl who was trying to quietly rearrange his equipment and stay in touch with the other units, said "Come on guys don't do this. Please don't do this." He had already figured out their plan.

Jerry and Ted went to Antonio's house and knocked on the door. Jerry pretended he was stoned. Antonio answered the door himself. Jerry said "Wow man, is that your T.A. out there?" "Yeah." "Whoa dude I am really sorry but the brakes on my van are fucked up and I clipped your right front fender when I pulled in." Ted piped up and said "No man, it was the left fender." "Oh yeah." Antonio was dressed in a Tee shirt, tight fitting sweat pants and socks. They noticed there was no way he was packing. They did not want him to go back inside. They hadn't decided if they should grab him right there or wait for a better opportunity. They were waiting to see what he would do. He said "Oh fuck." and streaked out in his stocking feet.

As soon as he got to the front of the car Jerry grabbed his left arm and threw him in an arm lock face down on the hood of the car. Meanwhile Ted had grabbed his other arm and had his gun out and screwed it into Antonio's ear. Jerry had a strong enough hold on Antonio so that he could have broken his arm. He told Ted to put his gun away and put the cuffs on Antonio. Meanwhile they saw several younger faces looking out the windows at them. They did not know if they were going to be attacked. The minute Earl saw Antonio come out of the house he had radioed homicide and as Ted was handcuffing Antonio the other units swarmed in. At least six cars were there in seconds.

They took control of Antonio. Their Sergeant gave Jerry and Ted a dirty look. Obviously not too happy with the way they had handled it. His people then stormed the house and secured the scene. Jerry said "Ok, we are out of here." They left. As they were driving off Ted said "He is going to fire some shit our way." Jerry said, "We got a successful arrest of a dangerous felon with no one hurt and the crime scene intact. Let him do his worst. He is a glory hound anyway. So who cares. The results speak for themselves."

When they got downtown Sergeant Ruffent said "You're back quick." Jerry filled him in and he said "Good job, don't worry 'bout nothin'. I got your back."

Ted and Jerry wrote their report. The next morning stories came out in the newspaper and guess who took the credit for going to the door and telling Antonio that they had hit his car?

Before Antonio was tried, there was a bail hearing coming up. Every person has the right to post bail unless just cause can be shown why they should not get it. That might be that the suspect was a flight risk or may have the intention to do harm to others. They heard that Antonio's father was gathering a large amount of money.

The entire unit went to the airport and with the help of the airport police checked every ticket office for reservation for all outbound flights leaving about the time Antonio would be released. They had them check under all the known aliases. They found tickets to Bolivia in one of Antonio's aliases. At that time the U.S. did not have an extradition agreement with Bolivia. One of the unit's men went to the Bolivian consulate and found out that Antonio had already been granted asylum there. Armed with the facts they presented this information to the court.

When Antonio's father showed up, a detective who was watching him overheard his attorney ask if he had the bail ready. The father answered "A cool million five right here." and slapped his brief case.

Once it was shown that he would flee, bail was denied. There was so much evidence that there was a very short hearing.

Two weeks later one of the unit's teams, that was assigned to organized crime activities such as bookies, race tracks and gambling, had gotten a warrant for a raid on one of the bookies they had been investigating for the last couple of months. The whole unit went on the warrant and after the arrests they collected evidence and ended up with boxes and boxes of paper work. They had to be careful of 'flash paper'. This was a type of paper that if even a spark hit, it would ignite all the paper and consume the entire stack in seconds. They often used this paper so that evidence would be destroyed if anyone else got hold of it. This was taken back to the office where the assigned team had to go through it and decide what would be put into evidence. These two men had an accounting background and were very competent. The process of weeding out the important financial material was extremely complicated.

While going through the paperwork they found a note indicating the mob was looking for an assassin to hit the following people. In order of priority, Antonio's judge, the prosecuting attorney, the assistant attorney and later Jerry and Ted. Fortunately it just went away after a while.

*   *   *   *   *   *   *   *   *   *   *   *   *   *

Jerry was teaching at the police academy. He taught a two hour course on Crisis Intervention. The whole purpose was to teach how to go into a high tension environment and defuse it without violence. To do that Jerry would describe scenarios and tell the recruits ways to defuse them without violence. There were fifty recruits and seated in the front row were six females. As he described each crisis and started to discuss the ways to resolve them the females would start in making comments like, "I'd kick him in the balls!" or "I'd rip out his Adams apple!" or "I'd kick his ass!" Then laugh and slap hands interrupting the class over and over.

After about an hour and a half, Jerry had enough. He said "I want everyone down at the gym seated in the bleachers, except you six ladies. You will go to the gym, dress in your P.Ts and meet me in the center of the gym floor." They asked, "Why?" Jerry answered, "I am going to kick all your six asses at the same time just to show you how tough you really are." They left right away and went to the office and bitched to the director. He came down to the gym and asked Jerry what was going on. Jerry told him and he said "What did you intend to do?" Jerry said he fully anticipated that all six would end up with at least four stitches by the time he got done. The director said "You can't do that." Jerry said "Sit down here and you can watch." He said "I can't allow that."

81

Then Jerry said "Fine, then I am out of here and don't call me again." That was the end of his teaching career.

One of the six came to work for him years later. She said that all of them were scared shitless and four of them cried. Only two of them made it through.

From the first affirmative action class, 65% were fired for failing to keep up scholastically. They filed a class action suit against the academy for racial harassment. The academy said they would no longer fire anyone even if they did not pass any of the tests.

*   *   *   *   *   *   *   *   *   *   *   *   *   *

About the same time period, the president of a large grocery distributor in south King County, came to the Sheriff and told him that a lot of their merchandise was missing. The inventory was way off and they suspected an inside job. They had tried to track it down but were not having any luck. They wanted help solving the problem. The Sheriff said that the undercover team could do it but only under certain conditions. First, no one else could be told about the investigation and second, they could press criminal charges. It seemed that often companies would rather just fire the employee than to take a chance of bad publicity.

The Sheriff called Jerry and Ted in and briefed them on the situation. They really had no place to start. They had no basic info or even suspicious individuals.

On the roof of the buildings there were huge flood lights shining down on each work area as well as the loading dock. Jerry and Ted went up on the roof to see if anyone on the roof behind the lights could be seen. The lights were too bright. They positioned themselves up there and took a LOT of photos of all the activity in the suspected area. They noticed the Foreman loading lots of food stuff in back of a trailer he pulled. He loaded case after case covering the bottom of his trailer then covered it with a pile of used cardboard and lashed it down. When he drove out the gate, security just thought he was taking the cardboard. Jerry and Ted took several photos of him doing so.

The crew at the dock loaded all the local delivery vans that took produce to various stores and business in the area. It soon became apparent that the foreman and three of the dock workers would take a case of something every few times and put it in the back of the foreman's trailer. About mid-week the Vice President of the company showed up at the loading dock and the foreman handed him a big wad of cash. Jerry and Ted got it all on film.

Just about the time the foreman was off work, they waited just outside the gate for him. They followed him, taking pictures. He would stop at taverns in Renton and take between 4 and 6 cases of coffee at each one. Then he went to a small town on the east side and delivered the rest to two stores there. They followed him for a week and he did this every week day. When they ran his name they found that the foreman had a prior for grand theft.

After a week they took all the photos and info to the prosecutor and got arrest warrants for all of them. Jerry and Ted went back in the morning and Jerry went into the Vice President's office. He knew the V.P. was due in at 9:00am. He showed his ID to the man's secretary and told her she was to say nothing to her boss other than good morning. When Jerry and Ted worked undercover they looked just like some guy on the street. He had to convince her that he was a policeman. He went into the man's office, sat down behind his desk and put his feet up on the desk. The man came in, said good morning to his secretary and walked into his office. He saw Jerry and yelled, "What the hell do you think you are doing? Jerry answered, "I think I am about to ruin your day." "Get your feet off my desk and get the hell out of here. Margi, call security."

Jerry took his feet off the desk, took his badge out and set it on the desk, "I think you need to sit down over here." "You ain't got shit on me!" Jerry started advising him of his rights and he kept trying to interrupt, "You got nothing on me, get out of here." Jerry started laying down 8" X 10" glossies but he was still flapping his lips. "That doesn't mean anything. You don't see me in these." Then Jerry flipped down the one of him accepting the money. His face went white. "I want my attorney." Jerry cuffed him and took him out to the van that was hauling the rest of the suspects. The foreman, however, was not there. It seemed he had gone on vacation and was hunting in Clockum Pass. That was of interest as he was a felon and not allowed to carry a firearm. The team knew there would be a ton of elk camps up there and would be hard to find him.

Jerry's department had a great relationship with Chelan County as they had done undercover work for them in the past and the folks there liked them. Jerry called the Sheriff there and told him about the guy and asked them to keep an eye out for him and arrest him. They told them that the guy was on the NCIC (National Crime Info Center) list. They said they would keep a look out for him. Well, unknown to Jerry, two of the officers said that they didn't have anything else to do that day so they would go out into the hunting area and "assist the game department" and look for him.

The very first hunting camp they pulled into who do they see but their guy walking along with a rifle over his

shoulder. They arrested him then Jerry and Ted drove over and picked him up. By the time they got back, they had a full confession and he had implicated the Vise President as well.

Jerry and Ted went to all the taverns and stores and each indicated that they had been buying for the last two years. None, however, admitted that they knew anything was stolen. They all claimed that they were told that it was company surplus that they were going to throw out. Jerry and Ted ran the numbers and discovered that they had taken the company for over $1,500,000.00.

The company was very happy with the teams work and became an ally in stopping other illegal activity by loaning the department anything they needed to solve a crime.

* * * * * * * * * * * * * *

The Green River Killer

The upper command was frustrated with the inability to solve the Green River killings. It seems every lead had gone cold. They requested Jerry's undercover team to run a twenty-four hour stake out on the man they suspected. His name was Gary Ridgeway. They did not have enough evidence to arrest him but were sure he was the one. Jerry's team did a moving surveillance on him twenty-four hours day for two weeks but during that time the man did nothing wrong anywhere. Part of that investigation involved getting "O and A's" (Offers and Acceptance) from prostitutes. Jerry's team would arrest them and tell them if they talked honestly to them they would let them go. The officers' main goal was to get any and all information they could about any weird men who picked them up. By this time the killer had already taken the lives of 28 women, mostly prostitutes. They talked freely to the officers but Jerry's team got no major information at that point. The upper command called them off.

It wasn't until much later that they caught Gary Ridgeway. By then they had recovered 48 bodies and he later confessed to killing twice that many. They were only able to catch him when they finally were able to analyze DNA sperm and tissue samples from the bodies.

*   *   *   *   *   *   *   *   *   *   *   *   *   *

There was a very large company that had a chain of outlet stores that sold just about everything. Cashgo in Tuckwillow, was having a problem with disappearing merchandise. The theft showed up in their inventory and bookwork but they couldn't trace the loss. They had been to the local Police department on two occasions but then the theft would stop. They were wondering if there was a leak somewhere. The president decided to come to Jerry's boss on his own in hopes of getting some "under-cover" help. Their Sheriff explained to this man about his two rules, before he would take it on. The man agreed.

The Sheriff called Jerry and Ted in and briefed them on the situation. They really had no place to start. They had no basic info or even suspicious individuals. They decided to do extensive back ground checks on all employees.   Two of the dock workers had minor charges on their records. They really needed an informant. They had to start somewhere. One of the dock workers lived in Lake Terrace so they checked with the local police. It seems that a year and a half ago, he had given some of his wife's prescription to a guy at a Tavern.   The guy was stopped for a DUI and had the pills in his pocket. This was not normally a case a prosecutor would take but was an arrest-able offence.

So they went to his house at 1:30 am and woke him up. They took him to the precinct to wake him up but soon realized that he never woke up. This was the state he was always in. Jerry told him that both he and his wife were going to jail unless he agreed to work with them. He finally agreed. He said that when a truck was unloaded they would run the receiver gun over most pallets but always "missed" one or two every so often. He said he had asked about it but was told it was none of his business. He noticed that every so often a pallet was set aside and left there maybe three or four hours. Later a pick-up with a tall canopy and covered widows would back up to the dock and two guys would take the stuff off the pallet and slide it into the canopy. The Dock Forman would get in and drive off with it.

Jerry and Ted set up surveillance on the dock and when the pick-up showed up, was loaded and drove off, they followed it to the Dock Forman's house. He had a very large garage/shop with two garage doors and one larger R.V. door. He would back in and two guys who were with him would unload the merchandise into his garage.

They followed him several times and on the third trip the Dock Forman took out a 22' tandem axel covered trailer and they loaded several loads and the pick-up on to the trailer. Friday night they drove off with Jerry and Ted following and went to Portland.

They went to a huge surplus supply warehouse. By now it was 3:00am. They met a man there and he and two helpers unloaded the trailer. Jerry and Bob documented everything. After the second trip they notified the Portland police and got a warrant for the warehouse as well as a Portland squad to help prepare a little surprise at the next delivery. The third delivery was made and unloaded. Just as the owner was about to lock up Jerry and Ted as well as the Portland squad rushed in. They took him back inside and using the Cashgo company scanner, they were able to identify all the merchandise stolen from that company. They identified over $100,000.00 of Cashgo items.

They arrested the owner for receiving stolen goods. He could not produce even one invoice for anything in the warehouse. He was informed that his sentence could be lighter if he cooperated with them and he agreed. He started talking and let it all out. Named names all the way up, including the Vice President of the company. They had nothing on the Vice President so they talked him into making a phone call that they could record.

He called the V.P. at 9:00am and started "ragging" at the V.P. He complained that he didn't get all the promised merchandise and was being overcharged. He also said that he did not get credit for the last payment he sent directly to the V.P. of $70,000.00. The V.P. got mad and shot back "What are you trying to do, scam me? I have a complete list of everything I sent you. And, I did give you credit for the entire $70,000.00. I don't want you to try and pull any shit on me. I keep precise records of everything that we give you and you signed for everything so don't try to jack me around." Then the owner said "I still think you are trying to scam me. I am going to watch a lot closer from now on." Jerry and Ted were very happy with that tape.

They went back to Seattle and the next time the dock foreman and his helpers loaded up and went to his house, they had a traffic stop lined up for them. They had a warrant for the truck, opened it up and arrested them for transporting stolen goods. They had the prosecutor waiting down town. Both were family men and rolled over right away. They said that the whole thing was the Vice President's idea and said he paid them to do it. He told them what to take and when then convinced them that with the volume Cashgo was doing they would never miss small amounts being taken.

Jerry and Ted got everything wrapped up legally by 10:00am and went back to Cashgo with four marked and two unmarked police cars making as big a show as possible. There must have been 100 or so employees watching as they arrested the Vice President and walked him out in hand cuffs. They also arrested the accomplices. One man on the loading dock tried to make a run for it but didn't get far. Jerry's boss was on the phone with the Tuckwillow chief explaining everything. The two dock workers spilled all and they found out about another man they did not know about and were able to catch him as well.

The Cashgo owner was very pleased with the results and told them if they ever needed anything to help solve a crime they would be glad to get it for them.

* * * * * * * * * * * * * *

A few weeks later, Jerry and Ted got a tip about a big store in Belleview that was buying and selling stolen electronic equipment. Jerry and Ted had a contact with a stereo manufacture in Seattle that would sell the police dept. units at wholesale so they could sell them as stolen to catch the criminals that were "fencing" them. They showed up at the store in Belleview and had a whole trunk load of stereos in the back. Jerry and Ted walked around the store, looking at everything but not buying just checking it out. A man came up to them, who matched the description they had of the boss and asked what they wanted. Jerry acted hesitant, looked around some more and finally asked, "If a guy was to show up with something to sell, what would he have to do, show I.D. or a sales slip or what?" The man was very cautious and asked a lot of questions. "Is it new? Is there a lot of it? Where did he get it?" Jerry went along and said "I have a friend that picks a warehouse and doesn't know how to move it." They talked about an hour, not getting specific, both being cautious. Meanwhile their electronic man, Earl, was outside in their old van listening and recording, over a wire, everything that was said.

Finally Jerry said "Look man, here is what we got." and told him. Then said "I want you to understand something, people who fuck with us don't hang around long." He looked at Jerry and Ted who were coldly staring at him and said "I believe you." Jerry said "Are you still interested." "Hell ya." Then they went out to the car and Jerry popped the trunk. The guy whistled and said "Shit, that's brand new. Where did you get that?" Jerry just looked at him, disgusted and said "Ah common man." He said "Oh yea, sorry man for asking." They negotiated a price for the trunk load. He asked if they could get more and if the serial numbers could be recorded?

When they did this kind of deal you have to say it was stolen. It has to be said plainly. Once said it often queered many deals. Otherwise the mark could say they didn't know it was stolen. Jerry said "You realize all this shit is hot man? So, you have to be careful how you deal it?" He got half offended, like they were questioning his intelligence and said "That's my end of the deal, I'll handle all that shit." Jerry was glad to hear him say that. He said "How much more can you get?" Jerry said "Our guy can only take so much out of each truck load." Then the guy gave them his card and said "Next time give me a call and let me know when you have some. How can I get hold of you?" Jerry said "You can't get hold of us, we will call you." He was getting a little leery of them.

A week later Jerry called him and said they had another load. They met him for lunch at a bowling alley. That made it hard for Earl to get everything on tape because of all the background noise, but he got most of it. The guy got to talking and asked what kind of other stuff they did. Ted said "Anything that makes us money, what you got in mind?" The guy hem hawed around some more than asked if they ever burglarized a place? Ted gave him a stupid look, like yea, sure were going to tell you that. He told them he was working on an idea for a job they could do that would be safe and they could pick up a couple of grand. Ted asked what and he said "Still working it out, I'll let you know next time." Jerry said "Ok" and then sold him their stuff and left.

The following week they met again for lunch. He had a big grin on his face and said" Oh I see the truck comes in once a week." Ted said "Don't try to get too smart man." That spooked the guy and he said "Hey man, sorry, didn't mean to snoop on your business, I'm sorry, really sorry, I am sorry." They talked generalities then he said "You know, I get the feeling that you are two of the badest fuckers I've ever dealt with." Jerry said "You don't know the half of it man." He said "I've got a deal I've been working on and I wonder if you guys could do it?" Jerry said "Don't know man, don't know what the deal is." He said "I been thinkin' about having my place burglarized. Then after stashing shit away somewhere, making an insurance claim on it. Then a couple of months later, selling it from the shop. There would be two grand apiece for you guys doing it. Jerry said "I don't know what about alarms and stuff?" He said "I am going to have alarm problems two days before this happens. My alarm won't be workin'." So Jerry said "Yea, you flesh it out and tell us next time and we can do it." He said "About a week?" They agreed and he said "I thought so."

The next week they brought another load, and met at the bowling alley. He wasn't interested in the stereos, just took delivery and paid them. He said "I have the burglary set up for two nights from now." It surprised Jerry and Ted that he had set it up so quickly. "Wow that was fast." "Well that's when I set it up and that's when you have to do it."

Jerry and Ted had done some undercover work for a large company that had employees stealing from them and they had been very pleased with the results and that company loaned them a van. They showed up at 2:00am on the planned date. The back door was unlocked and they went in and started loading up. The owner had told them what high end items he wanted them to take first and where they were in the store.

They loaded up the van and took the merchandise to a big warehouse barn he owned way out in the country. They were bitching the whole time about how much work it was. It was like moving a whole house load of furniture. Then the guy said it would be a week before he could pay them. Jerry got pissed and got right in his face. "You said we'd be paid tonight and tonight it is." "Ok man, ok man, don't get excited." He pulled money out of his pants and paid them. He muttered, "This is going to make me short for the week." Jerry didn't know why he did that, just trying to see if he could get away with it.

The next week Jerry called him and said they were bringing him another load. He said he didn't need any more stereos but wanted them to come over and talk to him. Jerry said "If we're coming over you can buy the stereos. He said "Ok, come on over, I'll buy the fuckin' things, just come over."

Jerry and Ted met with him again and he did buy the stereos. Then he asked if they could get anything else. Jerry said "Yea, what do you want?" He said "Big TVs" "Well how many do you want?" "As many as I can get." Jerry said "Have to be careful of that, we could get a whole fuckin' semi load." He had a look of disbelief on his face. "No shit? You can do a whole fuckin' semi load? Really a whole fuckin' semi load?" Jerry said "Yea, but it is a one time deal. Can you cover that?" He answered, "Fuckin' right, I want in." Jerry said "None of this pay next week shit. It's pay on the barrel head." He said "No problem." Jerry said "I can deliver them next week. Where do you want them?" He said "Right in my fuckin' driveway."

He made a mistake there, because he had never told them where he lived and Jerry made the mistake of not asking. However neither caught that. From surveillance, Jerry knew that he had a very large four car garage.

The company, that Jerry and Ted had done the undercover work for, didn't have enough T.V.s to fill a semi, so they packed the whole front with empty boxes and the back row was boxed T.V.s so it looked full. Jerry and Ted drove it to the guy's house and backed in to his driveway and opened the doors. He said "Holly shit, I didn't think you could do it. He wanted to look at everything right then, but Jerry said "No, money first." He said "Shit you guys don't trust anything." Jerry said "I trusted my mother once and she ran off with the guy next door." He cracked up laughing.

Jerry was beginning to wonder if this guy really had the money he said he did. Receiving payment for the stolen goods would seal the case for them. It was important to actually have the cash handed over to him.

This guy really liked them and thought they were a crook's dream come true. He reached into his pants pocket and pulled out a big wad of $100 dollar bills. He started to count them out and Jerry pulled out his wallet, flipped it open and said "Just put them in here."

He must have counted at least $1,000.00 before he noticed Jerry's badge on the other side of the open wallet flap.

Finally he noticed it and said "Man that is cool." Jerry said "Yea, it is." He said "Can you get me one like that?" Jerry replied, "I don't think so." "Why not?" "Cause you have to go to the Academy to get one." "What Academy?" "The police Academy." He stopped counting stood frozen looking Jerry in the eye. for about 40 seconds. "You're a cop?" "Yep." He stared at him another 30 seconds. "Really?" "Yep." and he just collapsed. Money scattered all around, just sitting there on the ground. He said "Oh shit, oh fuck man, oh shit." over and over, definitely in shock. Just kept repeating the same thing over and over. Jerry tried to get him to stand up and Ted was laughing so hard he couldn't get his breath. The man was so out of it that Jerry thought he would have to call an "Aid" cart for him. He finally stabilized and a patrol car took him away. They had to secure the scene, the truck, house and garage and a whole lot of paper work.

The man pleaded guilty to all charges. He also gave up the store in Moses Lake he was selling to. He had been pulling in hundreds of thousands a year.

*   *   *   *   *   *   *   *   *   *   *   *   *   *

One of the strangest cases Jerry was to investigate was one involving calls from three different farmers complaining of cattle mutilations. Jerry went to the farms, one at a time and looked over the scene. There was no blood, no footprints or tracks, even though in all three cases the ground was soft and damp. The farmer's footprints were there as well as Jerry's but nothing else. There was no sign that any attempt had been made to eliminate any tracks. All three cases were some distance apart but all in Carnation Valley.

In each case the jaw was cut out and the sex organs were removed and gone. No meat or any other part of the body was taken. Jerry thought it seemed likely that it was some kind of ritual killing. Something to do with a cult or black magic ceremony of some sort. He had no clues and although he talked to several people and groups he could not get any leads.

Then he heard about a witch's cult that was living at the end of Raging River Road. It seems there was a closed, gated community there. He drove to the area, there was a large gate and the whole area was surrounded by a tall fence. He opened the gate and went in. There were ten houses there so he went to the largest one in the center. He reasoned that it was most likely the home of the person in charge.

He knocked on the door and an attractive middle aged woman, dressed in a long gossamer dress with long sleeves and shoulder pads, answered. He identified himself and said that he needed to ask her some questions. She was very gracious, invited him in and <u>floated</u> to a sitting room. Yes, floated, it was really eerie, spooky. He could see no leg movement or any signs that she was walking, as though she were on a moving walk. A chill ran up his spine, how odd. Then she floated to the other room and came back with a cup of tea for him. It was like watching a sci-fi movie, unreal.

She answered all his questions and seemed to be very open and honest. She said that they did use goats that they purchased, to sacrifice in major ceremonies but never used cattle or any other animal. She had no idea who would do such a thing or for that matter why.

Although Jerry pursued every avenue he could, he nor the department ever were able to solve the case. There were no further mutilations. It is something that haunts him still.

Chapter 4
Going "Under" with the Motorcycle Gang

The next time Jerry met with the prosecutor and his attorney he told them about the requirement to become a club member. They told him that in order to commit a felony it could not be random. They would have to set something up ahead of time. They assured him that they could have the people ready to pull it off. That way the club would have no idea it was a set up. With this knowledge in mind he decided to meet with Mac again and let him "convince" him to become a prospect.

The next night he went to the bar and Mac came right over and shook his hand. He asked if he had been thinking about it and Jerry said "Well I am kinda interested in joining but I don't want to kill anyone. What do I gotta do?" Mac said "No man you do not hafta kill anyone. What would you be comfortable doin?" "Oh, I don't know" "What if I rob a gas station?" "That's cool, which one?" Jerry couldn't believe they were allowing him all this leeway. Jerry knew about one that was pretty isolated down town and suggested that one. Mac said "Well when do you want to do it?" Jerry answered, "How about midnight on Friday?" "That's cool we will have two of us with you to watch."

Jerry contacted the prosecutor and he said "Yea, we can set that up. We will have an undercover man there." Jerry said "It has to look violent, so have the guy pretend to resist and I will pretend to pistol whip him, then grab the money and run." "We can go for that and we will video tape it as well."

Jerry hung out with the club and strangely enough they seemed more nervous about it than he did. They kept saying things like, "Don't drink too much." "No drugs that night." "Gotta keep your shit together," etc. Finally Jerry said, "Take it easy man." "I am doing this, not you." They spent the rest of the time until Friday partying and "tickling women."

Friday night came and the club used an old beat up Plymouth 4 door that looked like shit that they used for stuff like this. The three of them got in and drove to the location. They parked about a fourth of a block away and watched through binoculars. Jerry thought pretty chicken shit, not very macho.

Jerry walked to the station and was surprised to see the guy that was there was the one chicken shit asshole cop that he hated most. This guy had cost him nothing but trouble and made no attempt to do anything right. He was a constant pain in the ass.

Jerry went inside and demanded money. The guy reached out for him, like he was supposed to, acting like he was resisting and Jerry hit him with his pistol. It was a 9-11.45. A heavy gun and Jerry hit him solid, dumping him. It actually felt pretty good to get back at him. He felt no remorse leaving him moaning on the floor. Jerry took the money and left. He just walked back to the car. Mac leaned out the window and said "Hey man, don't walk, run." "Why run, I guarantee, he's not going anywhere." Mac said "Fuck man, you nailed him." They went back to the club house and everyone was slapping him on the back and congratulating him. They got him a prospect jacket. It had a top rocker that said "prospect" and the bottom one that said where it was from, but no patch yet. Jerry said "I don't like to kiss ass I don't want to be a prospect long." Mac said "You won't be, we will rush it through."

Jerry was a "gofer" for about three weeks, then they told him they were going to have a "patching." They had a big party around a camp fire, gave him his patch, poured beer all over him, gave him hugs and kisses and spent the rest of the night partying. Evidently, some of the time, everyone pissed on the new member's patch, to "indoctrinate it!" Not Jerry's though.

Jerry supposedly conducted his business of buying and selling guns. The club wanted to see the guns and be able to buy them themselves. Jerry said ok, but let them know he could get three times as much from the radicals on the hill, so the club backed off.

There was a certain member who was a lot bigger than the others and carried a .380 in his vest pocket all the time. His nickname was "Roadblock." Nobody messed with him. Jerry was playing pool one evening and he came up and wanted the table and told Jerry to leave right away. The club expected members to stand up for themselves and short of killing the other, could do it any way they wanted to. Jerry said "OK, but you finish this last shot for me." He stepped back and when Roadblock bent over to take the shot Jerry jammed him against the table, reached into his pocket and took his gun and tossed it to another member. He said "Ok mother fucker we are going to see who backs down from who." Roadblock came up off the table and took his jacket off while Jerry did the same and they got into it. Jerry had been watching him for some time and noticed while he was big and strong, he was also slow and probably not a good fighter, he hoped. He was right and Jerry whipped his ass. The man didn't get in even two decent hits the whole fight.

The club president walked over and ripped Roadblock's name tag off his left chest and walked over to Jerry and said "This is the new "Roadblock." and handed Jerry the patch. Jerry thought the other man would be really pissed, but he took it well. Jerry never got any shit from him or any of his friends.

Over the next several weeks they spent a lot of time checking the night clubs and topless bars to make sure they were getting their percent for supplying the girls. They also went on rides to other areas and as far away as Montana, to visit other branches of the club. The officers would meet and discuss club business at that time. Of course most would attend the big meet at "Sturgis" each year, as well. In between they were selling a lot of drugs as well as a number of guns.

Within the first two weeks, Jerry had proof that the club was into dope and guns, as well as transporting women across the borders of Oregon, Washington and Alaska. He thought that once that info was passed on, he would be out of there. Then they had him buy a gun. It was a M I converted to full automatic. That was when the ATF and the FBI stepped in. They convinced upper command to keep Jerry in place for an indefinite time until the investigation was over. That turned out to be 18 months.

At that time the department posted a notice that Sergeant exams would be given. This was the first time in eight years this opportunity became available. It was also shortly after Affirmative Action was implemented. Applicants were told that the test would be based on information that could be found in eight books. Jerry submitted his name then bought all eight books. His friend Bart was having financial problems at the time and couldn't afford the books, so they studied together. They had a hard time as they had very little spare time. They often studied into the night some times over the phone. They had three months of intense studying before the day arrived to take the test. Jerry told the club that he had to go to California to help his sick sister so that he could get away long enough to take the test.

There were six hundred applicants. Bart actually finished #1 and Jerry finished with the 2nd highest score. The second part of the test involved an oral test in front of a panel. Anyone who scored seventy-five or higher on the written test, was eligible. When Jerry entered in his undercover persona they admonished him for coming that way. They told him he lost points because he didn't clean up first. He tried to explain why he was dressed like that with a beard and long hair working undercover, but they counted him down for it.

After the results were posted he was dropped to fourth place. The department promoted thirteen minorities with considerable lower scores. One of the minorities did not even pass the written test.

At the end of that time, the FBI, ATF and Jerry's department swooped in and arrested 34 members, including Jerry. Jerry supposedly made bail and got out. Quite a few of the others did as well. Then Jerry called them and said "Hey man, what the fuck is going on? What were you arrested for?" He was pulling it off for a while until the clubs attorney got a "disclosure" and found out that they were infiltrated. They put a hit on Jerry. Not for doing his job, but for violating the brotherhood.

He left the court house and was heading up James Street, cars were honking at a car going the wrong way and heading for him. He saw the gang's old Plymouth and a shot gun poking out the window, aimed at him. He jumped the curb, drove up the sidewalk and up the freeway on ramp just as his rear window was shot out.

Jerry drove clear to Olympia before he stopped and called to report it. He had called the com center in King County, but had to wait for a call back. Sheriff Dave called back and talked with him for 30 or 40 minutes getting all the information he could, including the names and any other facts Jerry had on the club officers. Then he asked Jerry if he had any relatives in the area? Jerry said "No, but I have some in Salem." The Sheriff told him to go visit them for 3 or 4 days and he would call him there. Then Jerry got drunk with several of his state patrol friends, and spent the night in Olympia with one of them. The next day he went to Salem.

Jerry came back a few days later and met with the prosecutor and his attorney. They were still concerned about the "Hit." They said it would be a least six weeks before the first hearing that would require his presence. They advised him to get out of the area and not tell anyone where he was going. They were able to convince his boss that he needed a vacation after 18 straight months of work.

Jerry's new boat was a 32' Blue Water sail boat with

an inboard 36 HP 3 cylinder Volvo motor. He loaded up and left for Canada. He had been there several times in the past, fishing, and never had problem going through customs. Having traveled there so many times he knew their M.O. well. When he came into the harbor he saw them going for their "jump suits" and thought, WOW! Someone is going to get their boat trashed. Their authority is scary. They could cut everything up, give it back in pieces and say "Ok you're fine you can go." UH, OH! They were going for him. Then he looked in the mirror. "Jeeze, I look like a dope dealer." He realized that the inspectors would not recognize him the way he looked now. He pulled up to the dock, jumped out, tied up and met them half way down the dock. "Hey I know what you are coming for, here is my ID and badge, "I look like this because I am working under cover." They looked his ID over closely then they all went back to Jerry's boat and enjoyed several drinks with him, shot the shit for three hours and had a great time.

Jerry often worked with the Canadian Mounties, teaching classes about motorcycle gangs and what was happening in the states. He always enjoyed their company. To him this was another example of the great people there. He was cleared and went to a small island for the night. The next day he went on to Nanaimo and spent two days there.

The first night he went to the local bar and as he was enjoying a beer, a drunken Indian came up and demanded money. Jerry said "Go away, I won't give you any money." The guy was getting louder and pushing Jerry, "Gimmy some money now." "Look man, I don't want to hurt you, go away and leave me alone." The man kept at him and Jerry looked around the bar and asked if anyone knew him and could get him to leave. All the locals just ignored him. Jerry was getting pissed as he just kept it up, so he put a hammer lock on the guy and walked him outside then came back in.

Minutes later the guy was right back. Jerry asked out loud, "Hey I don't want to hurt this guy, he is obviously drunk. Does anyone know who he is?" No answer, then the guy pushed him and tried to reach his pocket. Jerry punched him and the guy went down. Jerry caught him and took him out again and told him to go home and sleep it off. Jerry wasn't back in more than a few minutes when the guy came back in and got right in Jerry's face demanding money, Jerry had taken all he could and hit him in the solar plexus, the guy doubled over, ran out and puked his guts out. He finally went home. All of a sudden everyone was Jerry's friend. They were all buying him drinks. It seems the whole thing was some kind of test the Canadians used to measure Americans.

That night Jerry met a guy and his wife at the bar and they really hit it off. By the next morning he had invited them to go out on his boat and the wife brought her sister for Jerry. They got out in the ocean and Jerry then found out that they were nudists. They did not put their clothes back on unless a boat came close or they had to go in for supplies. They were out for two weeks and had a grand time. They had to go back to work, so he took them in, restocked the boat and went out again to Desolation Sound. He had a great time for the next several days fishing, lounging around and sun bathing. There was a great afternoon wind almost every day.

Jerry was also a professional scuba diver and did small jobs on the side, on Lake Union, Lake Washington, in the sound and at one time on Lake Sammamish, to recover a lost outboard motor to make extra money. He had a small sign on either side of his boat with a diver's flag, a red square with a white slash across it and "Another Underwater Service", written on it.

When Jerry went back in to gas up and get water, one of the dock owners approached him after seeing his sign and asked for his help. It seems that he had a broken underwater water line. PVC pipe brought fresh water from a spring in the hills to the dock and it was leaking.

He said he would give Jerry $500.00 to fix it. He said he didn't care if it took five hours or five days he would pay $500.00. Jerry agreed, suited up and dove down.

He found that someone had dropped an anchor on the line and broke it. The man had to go to the other side of the bay to turn the valve off, then Jerry had to

scrounge everything he could to float the section of pipe to the surface so that he could fix it. He found inner tubes, little parachute devices that held air and anything else that would float. It was finally fixed then he got it back down. The guy had a number of old fishing net buoys, so Jerry tied lines to them, then tied them all along the water pipe so that boats could see where the line was.

The owner was very pleased and was more than happy to pay him. As he was loading his gear another man came up and said he had a 40' boat and had hit some rocks and wanted Jerry to check it for damage. Jerry found the rudder damaged but was only able to wire it up until the guy could get his boat out of the water to fix it.

The guy at the marina thought he would do Jerry a favor and put it out over the air that they had a working diver there. He got all kinds of calls. He had 10 tanks and he kept busy for two solid weeks. He had to go back to Nanaimo for more air and had twelve more calls waiting for him when he got back. He got to thinking, I am supposed to be on vacation, this is NOT a vacation. He told the folks there he would do the next ones they had right then, but did not want to take any more jobs. He earned over $4,000 in that short time.

Jerry spent the next few weeks fishing and enjoying his boat. He was a good fisherman and would trade his extra Salmon for Whiskey or snacks. He really enjoyed the wonderful friendly folks and the great fishing.

When the time came to go back, he sailed down the coast to Friday harbor to check into customs. It was a little spooky as he had $5,000 Canadian and two cases of Whiskey. He was thinking that it may be more than he could legally take back. He wasn't even sure if it was legal for him to have worked there.

As he pulled near the custom's dock he saw a space that he could tie up. Then some guy started jumping up and down yelling at him and waving his arms. He wasn't close enough to hear what he was yelling and wondered if he was trying to hold a place for someone at the dock. That is not allowed. He continued to yell and wave his arms then Jerry was close enough to hear what he was yelling. "You can't come in here, there isn't enough room. You're going to hit my swim step." He was the owner of a 50' Chris Craft. Jerry knew better. He knew where his boat would fit so he ignored the man. The guy was getting madder and madder.

Meantime Jerry just slid in and tied up adding an extra spring line to keep his boat from drifting into the other boat. The man was yelling, "You stupid son of a bitch, if you hit my swim step I'll sue you, you ass hole." He was being a real prick.

While Jerry was bent over tying his boat the guy came up behind and leaned over him yelling at him even though he could see Jerry's boat was not touching his. Jerry stood up, turned around, grabbed the man by his shoulders, lifted him off his feet, walked over and held him over the water. The guy got really quiet. Jerry said "I just spent six weeks in Canada with some of the nicest, warmest most accommodating people you would ever

104

want to meet. When I come home, the first American I meet is an asshole like you. Then Jerry dropped him in the water. He stayed to be sure the guy got out all right but didn't help. The man climbed out of the water, ran back to his boat, jumped inside and what must have been his son jumped out and came toward Jerry. He took one look at Jerry and got back in their boat and closed the door and the curtains.

A customs agent, a man about 60, was sitting outside smoking. As Jerry walked up he said "Oh, giving swimming lessons I see." Jerry said "Yea, just thought he needed to cool off." The customs man said "Yea, I think so too." Then they stamped his book and sent him on his way.

It took two days to sail to Seattle, when he pulled in to his space and plugged in, he called the prosecutor and told him he was back then called the Sheriff. They arranged to meet and the Sheriff told him that he had called in the S.W.A.T. team and that they went to the club house, took the President, Vice President and the Master of Arms into custody and took them down town to the Sheriff's Office. The Sheriffs then told them in minute detail what would happen to them if anything happened to Jerry. He went on to say that he didn't care how or what happened, but if anything did, it would still happen to them, their families and the club. Then he called in the S.W.A.T. team and said "Take them to the basement and show them what I mean. They were then taken to the hospital and stitched up and taken back to the club house. Two days later the contract was removed. This was one awesome Sheriff that would go this far to protect his men.

It was about a week and a half before the first hearing took place. He did get a lot of dirty looks and a occasional middle finger but no threats. The prosecutor was hoping they would threaten him as they could win a stiffer sentence. There were thirty four separate trials and they were held over a period of eight to nine months.

During this period they did not want to assign duty to Jerry so that he could maintain his disguise. So, they had him take an extended vacation. He went to work for a sail boat dealer on Lake Cut, as a "boat rigger". This involved installing instruments, sails and rigging. Meanwhile he lived on his 32' boat. The man that had a small sail boat in the slip next to him became a buddy and they often partied together. One day he went to the boat dealer where Jerry was working and ended up buying a 32' sail boat.

He wanted to have a party to "christen" his new boat. The plan was to start at Jerry's boat then have him make a grand entrance sailing into the slip next to him. He was to pick up the boat on Friday evening. He bought several cases of beer and champagne and stored them on Jerry's boat.

By 5:00pm on Friday guests started arriving. There were about sixteen people there. Two women friends showed up and had already been to three other parties. They were pretty "buzzed". The women, Katy and Sara were having a grand time. Jerry's friend called and said he would be a little late but everyone was having a good time and didn't mind. When he did come sailing in everyone clapped and cheered. The party then moved to the new boat. As the evening wore on Jerry's date had to leave, and most of the other guests left as well.

The few that were left decided to go to a restaurant for a late dinner. Katy and Sara, who were feeling no pain by this time, decided that they wanted to go to a movie. Both were too drunk to drive and they couldn't talk them out of going, so Jerry said he would take them to the movie so everyone else could go to dinner. He drove them there and had to hold both of them up so they wouldn't fall down walking to the theater. They were only inside a short time when Sara fell asleep. Afterwards, he took them back to his boat and fed them coffee to sober them up. Katy sobered up first and was able to drive home. Sara was still in bad shape so they just sat around and talked to 5:00 am. They started dating and after some time Jerry asked her to marry him. They were married shortly after his promotion.

*   *   *   *   *   *   *   *   *

Chapter 5
A Promotion

Jerry was still in his undercover persona. The trials were scheduled and he had to maintain it until then, so that the jury would understand how he was able to infiltrate the gang.

Jerry was finally promoted several months later, on the next to the last day that applicants could be promoted from that list.

When Jerry made Sergeant they did not want any of them working with people they knew. He was sent to the south west part of the county. He was assigned to the swing shift. Two of the men on his crew had been on the force for twenty years. They were very competent officers but not aggressive. They didn't go looking for trouble but if anything happened they would handle it well and correctly. For a young aggressive officer like Jerry it was frustrating at times. However he knew he could always count on them to do a good job.

These two were always talking about duck hunting and often went on their days off. One day they asked Jerry if he would like to go. Jerry said he would. Then one morning at 5:45am he got a call from an irate citizen who said that two policemen were hunting on his private duck pond. Jerry asked how he knew they were police men. He said because they parked their police cars right in front of his house, got waders out of the back and then their shot guns. Jerry gets there and the first thing he sees is the police cars with both shot guns missing. Jerry thinks, "For Christ sakes, hunting with department guns, with department cars while on duty, this keeps getting worse and worse."

Jerry goes to the house and knocks on the door. The owner comes to the door and is very angry. He said that the two policemen got out of their cars, got waders out of the back and put them on then got their guns and went to his private duck pond. Jerry is thinking, "My God, how am I going to get these guys out of this without having them fired. They are throwing their whole career away to hunt ducks. He is really stressed out. He asks the owner which way the pond is and he says just over the hill. Jerry said "I will handle this, don't worry." He starts to walk in the direction the owner indicated. The owner said "Wait a minute, it is really muddy. You can't walk over there in those shoes. Come on in and I will loan you some boots. I have some here in the mud room." Jerry goes inside and sits down and starts to take his shoes off. Just then his two officers walk out of the next room laughing. It was all a set up. It seems the owner is a retired cop who now is a butcher and helped them put it together. He said "How about some duck coffee?" and that led to further duck jokes. Jerry had to admit they got him good.

About six months later Jerry was working grave yard. He had stopped at the fire station and was having coffee with his friends there. They were cleaning house and had an old "Rescue Annie". A training doll for CPR classes. It was worn out and not worth repairing. Jerry asked if they were going to throw it away and they said they were. He asked if he could have it. He was coming up with a plan. He knew of an area that had been purchased for development nearby. There were three or four old houses there that were given to the fire department for training fires. He got the addresses and was told that it would be two weeks before they burned them. He went to his butcher friend and asked him for some pig intestines and some blood. Of course he had to tell him the plan and make him swear to keep quiet. The butcher loved the idea and went along.

Jerry went to one of the houses that would be burned and put the Annie down, put the pig intestines by her stomach and blood all around. Then he stuck an ax in the floor by the "body". Next he walked in the blood and left foot prints going out to the porch and down the steps.

Then he called the com center supervisor and got him to help with the set up. He knew the older one, Don who was one of the two that set him up, carried a cheap flash light that was not very bright. Jerry and his supervisor got dispatch to call Don and send him out to respond to a woman screaming at that address.

When Don got there the first thing he sees is the bloody foot prints. Not wanting to contaminate the crime scene he touches nothing and shines his weak flash light inside. He sees the body against the far wall, with the intestines and blood all around. He knows she is dead. He goes back to his car and calls for homicide and his sergeant, Jerry. Jerry calls back and says, "Hold off on the homicide call, I'm in route." He pulls up, gets out of the car and Don is really excited and almost babbling. Jerry said "Calm down, wait a minute, let me look." He goes to the door and shines his flash light in then walks back to his car, gets in and starts it up. Don says, "What are your doing?" Jerry says, "For Christ sakes Don, it's just a woman." He puts the car in gear and drives off. Don's mouth is hanging to his chest. He was in shock for thirty seconds before he caught on. Don gets on his radio and says "I'll be clear, prank one." Then he called Jerry and said "Pretty good get back."

As a Sergeant, Jerry was supervising twelve to twenty-five patrol cars. There was never a shift that something unusual, notable or stressful did not occur. There was no such thing as a "Easy Day". He was in the office when a call came in about a drunk driver killing five children. He rushed to the scene as quickly as possible. A state patrolman was already there and the Fire Department Medic crew was just ahead of him. It seems as though a 22 year old woman who spent the morning partying and was now staggering drunk was headed home and driving 80 to 90 miles per hour had missed a curve, plowed 75 feet off the road and through a picket fence into a child day care center. She killed five children and injured three others.

The State Patrol officer had arrested and hand cuffed her and was trying to put her in the back of his car. She was cursing and trying to kick him while fighting him all the way. He finally got her in the back of his car and shut the door. Then he and Jerry started over to help the Firemen medics with the children. Jerry glanced back at the car and the woman had gotten out of the cuffs, out of the car and was running away. The State Patrolman ran after and caught her, re-cuffed her and was bringing her back. Now Jerry knew that the State officers while attending their academy were taught to be as courteous as possible, not to be "rough" and to maintain good public relations, to handle each situation with "kid gloves." Jerry went to the car and checked the cuffs. She had been able to get out of them the first time because they were way to loose. Jerry tightened them.

He shut the car door and started to go to the children and she started kicking the car window as hard as she could while screaming every fowl word she could at them. Jerry said "Hog tie the bitch." The state office said "Oh my God, we aren't allowed to do that." Jerry said "Well I sure as hell am." All street officers carry a short piece of rope with a loop on one end and a snap on the other. He jerked her out of the car, put the loop around her ankles, tightened the loop then fastened the snap to her hand cuffs and put her back in the car.

When Jerry and the State Patrol officer got to the medic's van, two of the firemen were sitting on the back bumper crying uncontrollably. Seeing the dead bodies of the five children was horrible, Horrible. Everyone at the scene would have nightmares.

The woman who owned the day care center said cars were speeding on their frontage road all the time. She had called the highway department several times to report it and ask for help but nothing was ever done. The woman driver was charged with a DWI and multiple vehicular homicides and went to jail for a long time.

A few days later Jerry called the traffic department to find out what was being done. They said it was on the list but they "hadn't gotten to it yet." Jerry decided to detail one of his cars to work that road with radar. It was interesting to note that of the several tickets they issued, one was to the ambulance driver who had picked up the children. He was driving his private car and was driving 15 mph over. He was very embarrassed.

*   *   *   *   *   *   *   *   *   *   *   *   *   *

One young rookie after passing the program was assigned to respond to a call that came in, to check the welfare of an eighty two year old woman. Her porch light had been on for several days and in the past she had turned it off every morning. The neighbor, who usually picked her up every Wednesday to take her shopping, said that when she knocked the woman did not answer the door. The neighbors were worried about her. Jerry heard the call he told dispatch that he was nearby and would observe to see how the rookie handled it.

When they got there all the doors were locked. They went around the entire house and knocked loudly on all the doors as well as the window to her bedroom. There was no answer. They could see that everything was clean and neat and there was no sign of a break in. The rookie did not know how to get in, so Jerry told him they would have to break in. Jerry first asked the neighbors if one of them would fix the door if the, broke in and one of them agreed.

The rookie tried to kick in the garage door, feeling that less damage would be done there. He kicked it as hard as he could but it did not give. Jerry said "I'll show you how it is done." He gave the door a tremendous kick but nothing happened. Now he was embarrassed and offended. He felt foolish, so he kicked it again as hard as he could. There was a very loud clang, clang, clang. She had installed an angle iron across the inside of the garage door. When they got to the inner door the rookie kicked it and it shattered. They went in yelling, "Hello, hello, we are the police, we are here to help you, are you ok?" No answer. When they got to the bedroom, they found her on her queen sized bed that was shoved up against the wall. She was lying in a fetal position, facing the wall and hadn't moved despite all the noise they made. There was an odor of a day old body.

The rookie said "I will call the medical examiner to come and get the body." Jerry said "NO, you check the body for a pulse, levity and trauma." The rookie said "Ah Sarge, you are fuckin' with me." Jerry shot back, "Bullshit, I am teaching you to do the job right. If you don't want to do it right, we'll have a long talk about it later. You don't ever assume anything."

The rookie got on the bed on his hands and knees and crawls over to the body. He reaches out and put his hand on her neck to feel her jugular vein to check her pulse. She bolts up and starts screaming at the top of her lungs. The rookie rose up on his knees and he starts screaming also. Both of them are screaming at each other. Jerry is doubled over laughing. No one told them she was deaf.

It seems she had the flu for the last few days and that was why she hadn't been out. Jerry couldn't stop laughing and had to go outside to keep from hurting any feelings. He left the rookie to explain why they were there. When he went out all the neighbors were waiting to hear about her health. He could barely contain his laughter long enough and told them she was ok and would be out shortly. He had to go sit in the car until he could stop laughing.

* * * * * * * * * * * * * *

He was on the street with his crew when they got a domestic violence call. This was from a house they had been to before. The man there had been arrested in the past for domestic violence and resisting arrest. Two units responded, going to the front and Jerry, who was in the area, called and said he would take the back door.

This was a long narrow house on a slope with a deck above the basement in the back. There were steep stairs going to the deck and the main part of the house. Jerry could see that someone was building a retaining wall as there were concrete blocks, pilled dirt, shovels and a wheel barrow scattered around on the ground below the deck. Jerry climbed the stairs and was passing in front of the door to get on the open side.

All of a sudden, the door exploded. The suspect crashed through the door with no attempt to open it and right into Jerry. The door, Jerry and the suspect crashed through the railing and over the edge, nineteen feet to the ground. Jerry landed on his side with the wind knocked out of him. He was stunned and disoriented. He couldn't move. He was immediately concerned that the suspect might try to kill him but he couldn't get his eyes to focus. He tried desperately to control his vision. When he was finally able to see, the suspect was lying next to him on his side facing Jerry with his eyes open. About one half of his brain and his skull cap were on a concrete block and the rest of his head was shoved up against it. Jerry thought, "Well, he's not going to hurt me."

Jerry heard his guys running toward him, and then passed out. The next thing he knew the Medic crew was there and took him to the hospital. The odd thing was Jerry was not aware of any pain until the shock wore off. Then his neck and shoulder felt as though there was a car parked on it.

When he got to the hospital the doctor had him X-rayed at once. They found a broken collar bone, broken rotator cup, broken scapula, three broken ribs, two broken fingers, torn muscles and torn ligaments. They were relieved and surprised that there were no spine injuries as he experienced a lot of pain in his neck.

Jerry was rushed to surgery and the doctor operated for six hours. Later the doctor told him that the damage was more extensive than he thought. He wasn't sure Jerry would ever recover enough to go back to work. Jerry said "Oh yeah? Just watch me."

When Jerry had to have surgery it required a period of recuperation. He was assigned as a communications supervisor. This was a big job. He had thirty-five employees most of whom were women. It seemed that some of them were bitching all the time. He managed to work with them and they at least respected him. It took a year before his doctor released him.

When Jerry was finally able to see if he could return to active duty the doctor was there to test him. He had a sixty-five pound barbell and told Jerry to pick it up with one hand while standing straight, curl it then raise it over his head, then down to his side with no surges. He had to do that four times. Then he was told to put it on the floor wait sixty seconds and repeat this three times. When Jerry completed the exercise, the doctor said "This is an amazing recovery considering the amount of damage that was done."

He was aware that Jerry had worked very hard in rehab to get these results. Jerry said "Well, did I pass?" The doctor said "Oh - - you passed on the first four. I just wanted to see how determined you were." Jerry laughed and said "You prick." The doctor laughed as well and signed the release papers, clearing him to go off light duty.

When his rehab was just about over, the Commander of the Criminal Investigation Unit asked him to take over the Narcotic Division. When he spoke to his wife about it she was frightened for him and asked him not to. He was also hesitant as there seemed to be a lot of politics involved. He told the Commander that he was not interested in doing so.

*   *   *   *   *   *   *   *   *   *   *   *   *   *

A few months later Jerry was called into the Sheriff's office. This was a man that Jerry and everyone else admired. He came up through the ranks and was highly qualified. The kind of person you would give 100% for, without being asked. He was a cop's cop. He was head of the Sheriff and Police Chief Association of the State of Washington. Dave was 5' 9", with an average build, a good dresser, with an air of authority but understood what the guys in the field were going through. He made no unreasonable rules. His rules were well thought out and were followed to the letter. He had complete loyalty. Cops are always bitching about something but you never heard any complaints about Dave.

When Jerry got to his office, Dave poured him a cup of coffee, the whole softening up routine. Jerry knew he was up to something. Dave wanted to know why Jerry didn't want to work narcotics. Jerry said "I know about all the politics involved in criminal investigation and frankly I just don't want any part of it." Dave said "How about if I cut a deal with you?" This was when all the hackles on Jerry's neck went up. He had a pretty good idea what was coming and didn't see a way to get out of it. Dave went on, "How about if you work directly for me. You don't answer to anyone else." Jerry answered, "Isn't that political suicide for me?" "I thought you weren't interested in politics?" The sucker had him. He out foxed Jerry and had him from the get-go.

Dave knew what Jerry was going to say before he said it and knew he had him. Jerry asked him how it would work. "You would answer only to me. I trust you to be able to run it right. The only thing I don't want is to ever be surprised. I would want weekly briefings, no names of suspects, just a general idea. If anything goes wrong, I want a phone call right away." Jerry couldn't find much to argue with. Everything Dave requested was reason-able. He said "Let's discuss what really needs to be done, but I don't really like the idea." That didn't seem to bother Dave at all.

The second time that Jerry met with Dave they discussed some concerns about a state law that they felt should be changed. At the time, the law stated that all proceeds from drug seizures would be split up between the state Police Officer training center and the County general fund, to be spent as the County Executive desired. When the drug enforcement unit was formed the budget was $50,000 per year. It consisted of six detectives and one sergeant. It was never increased. Dave and Jerry agreed that the law needed to be completely changed to include additional officers, supervisors and funding.

Dave called the financial executive of the police department and they met to discuss it. The three of them came up with a plan. They campaigned at the state capital and met with the state representative and introduced a bill that would state that 50% of all funds received from drug related seizures would revert back to the seizing agency to be used for drug enforcement only. The other 50% would continue to go to the state Police Officers training center.

The three of them decided that to be able to gain extra personal, they had to get the public behind them. They agreed that getting publicity would put pressure on the county executive to provide added man power. Now they needed to put their plan to work.

A short time later, Jerry found out that the person he was replacing was the same officer that he had replaced when he first made detective. When Jerry found out he was amazed. He couldn't imagine a less qualified person if he stayed up all night thinking about it. How the heck did that jerk ever get in? Now the guy went from just not liking Jerry to hating his guts.

The man was constantly berating Jerry and tried to take credit for several things that Jerry did for the next several months. Anyone with half a brain could see what was going on and everyone in the department knew he was a piece of shit. They just did not like that guy.

The man had hired three men who did nothing but kiss his ass. They were as worthless as he was. Jerry didn't want to storm in and start firing people, so he decided to give the three of them enough rope to hang themselves. And, they did.

Jerry had a private meeting immediately upon arriving, with his top three detectives. These were the men that were doing all the work and getting none of the credit. He told them that they would be working with him as a four man unit and were not to divulge anything to the other three. He told them that if they had a search warrant they were not to say anything to those three until they were suiting up to serve the warrant. He went on to tell them that the reason for this was because they would tell their ex-boss who would pretend that it was one of his cases. Jerry said that he suspected that that man was giving information to other jurisdictions in an attempt to screw up their warrants.

At that time, there was controversy about whether "head shops" were legal or not. What was to say that the paraphernalia was not used to smoke tobacco?

One of the three ass kissers went on a campaign and without saying anything to Jerry, went to the Prosecutors' office and got them to issue a warrant on a head shop. Supposedly the Prosecutor agreed to do so as a test of the state law. They wanted to see if it was legal or not.

The ass kisser came to Jerry with that warrant and wanted the unit to serve it. Then he tried to pull the big one. He said that the Prosecutor made a special request and asked for him and his two partners by name to be visible serving the warrant as they had more experience. The Prosecutor had supposedly wanted media coverage as well to let the public know they were closing in on offenders. Jerry knew that was a lie. He told the three of them to go ahead set it up and run with it. The rest of the unit would be involved in another case that couldn't be delayed. Then Jerry told everyone else that no matter what happened stay the hell away from that warrant. They all ended up at the other end of the county and did indeed have a case there.

The ass kissers went to the north end of the county to serve the warrant. They spent the entire day packaging glassware, showing the press what they were doing, getting their faces on T.V. and in the paper and making a grand stand play. Wow, look at us. The guy that Jerry replaced was taking credit and said he had masterminded the whole plan.

The next day, Jerry went to the Prosecutor's office and met with the Prosecutor who had written the warrant. Jerry asked, "Whose idea was it to get this started?" The Prosecutor said "You guys. If you guys hadn't lobbied so hard it wouldn't have gotten done." Jerry asked, "Who specifically was doing the lobbing?" His eyes got big and he said "Uh oh, I see shit in the water!" Of course it was one of the ass kissers who had been there. Jerry asked the Prosecutor if he had specifically requested any detectives by name, to assist the one who got the warrant. He answered, "You know better than that. We can't tell you who to send on a warrant. I had a tough time getting the warrant signed as no one was comfortable with that law.

Because the detective kept hounding me I finally convinced the judge that the law needed to be tested and I finally got the warrant."

Jerry went back to this office and called a meeting with the man. He asked him to reiterate the story. The little dumb ass should have seen it coming but he didn't. He claimed that the Prosecutor had come to him due to his extensive experience and had wanted experienced men on the warrant. That is why the Prosecutor wanted his two friends with him. Jerry asked, "Is everything you told me exactly the way it happened? Are you sure you don't want to change anything?" The man should have taken the clue. He answered "Nope, that's just the way it happened." Jerry said "That's what the Prosecutors said? Funny, because I just talked to him and that is not what he told me." He tried to argue. Jerry said "Should I call him and have him come down to this meeting?" The man declined.

"You have one hour to clean out your desk and get out of here. North precinct is expecting you. You're going back on the street. Oh, and on your way out, send your two buddies in here." The three of them put their heads together in the hall then came in. One of them said "I guess you want us out of here too?" Jerry said "Just as fast as you can."

* * * * * * * * * * * * * *

When Jerry first took over, he had a meeting with the unit. He explained what he expected out of them and what his rules were. He was working directly for the Sheriff and didn't need anyone's permission to hire or fire anyone. He had no political coat tails to hide under. His rules were simple and reasonably easy to follow:

1. Everyone had to be to work on time.
2. Everyone had to be completely accountable for everything they did. If you make a mistake, in good faith, come to me immediately with it and between us we'll take care of it. But if it's a stupid mistake or on purpose you will eat the consequences of it.

Jerry's hard fast no debate instant transfer rules.
1. If you lie to me you're gone
2. If you have sexual relations with an informant, you're gone.
3. If you steal narcotics or money you're gone.

Once they were gone Jerry brought in three really great guys. He stole one from Auto theft, one from Training and took one as a personal favor to upper command staff. This guy turned out to be an excellent officer and a great asset to the unit.

Sometime later Jerry met with the Chief of the Airport Police. He decided to take Tony, with him. Tony was in his mid-30's, 5' 11" and a skinny 145 lbs. He looked 50. He had bags under his droopy eyes, a thin face, a gruff voice and could buy dope in a Mormon church on Sunday. He was so good and worked so fast that Jerry had to hire someone else to do his paper work so that Tony could keep going. He was Jerry's best.

They drove to the airport in a red Corvette undercover car to meet with the Chief of the airport police. When the meeting was finished, they left his office

walking into the terminal. They immediately saw two young Mexican men walking in front of them speaking Spanish. Their airline tickets were stuck in their pockets and they had just gotten off the plane.

Jerry's unit had made a big arrest the prior week involving a Mexican gang. They arrested 25 suspects, recovered a kilo of Heroin, $200,000 in cash, 12 cars and 3 houses.

Tony said "I betcha that's the new crop." Jerry said "You wanna see? Go get the car and met me at the taxi area." Jerry followed the two men to the baggage area then out to the cab stand. They hailed a cab and pulled out.

Toni pulled up behind them and picked up Jerry. They followed the suspects who went directly to a car lot that was known to sell a lot of cars to the Mexicans they had arrested. The two Mexicans got out and looked at different cars. They seemed especially interested in two Camaros, a blue one and a yellow one.

Jerry and Tony had parked across the street and were walking along the sidewalk watching them. On a whim Jerry yelled across to them, "Hey, buy the blue one." They did. When they left the car lot in the Camaro

120

Jerry and Tony followed them to a house that was unknown to the detectives. The two men got out, unloaded their bags and went in. Tony then called one of his informants and told him to order a 16th. (16th of an ounce of heroin.) Then Jerry called the office and scrambled the guys while telling them where they were and to take up positions in a two block radius around them.

When it was all set up they only had to wait about 30 minutes. The two men came out. Jerry and Tony followed them while leap frogging with other undercover detectives straight to the delivery point that had been set up. The unit rolled in on them blocking their car on all sides with guns drawn. The arrest was completed before the two men knew what was happening.

Jerry always had his crew come in hot and heavy. Being so aggressive resulted in fewer shootings and fights. They scared the shit out of the suspects before they could react. They secured the dope, the car and both men. Their search warrant writer wrote a warrant for the house on the way to the judge's office while his partner drove. After the judge signed the warrant the unit stormed the house and found a soft ball sized chunk of heroin, over $100,000 in cash, several machetes, several guns and five other suspects. This unit was so effective that they had the whole scene secure in sixty seconds with no shots fired. Jerry did not like daylight warrants as it is harder to come out of them without a shooting, but this one went well.

There were three types of warrants. #1 was a tweeker. It was issued for dealers of speed, cocaine, methamphetamine, Ritalin and illegal pharmaceuticals. These people were highly unpredictable, violent, armed and dangerous. When serving this warrant they always went it as hot and heavy as possible knowing they could be killed. #2 was issued for a Heroin raid. These people were more mellow, but possible violent, possible armed and were likely to resist arrest.

When serving these warrants they went in fairly hot unless it was a day time warrant. Serving a warrant during the day was more dangerous as the suspects were alert. #3 was issued for a marijuana growing operations. These people were laid back, with a good time Joe attitude. Usually not violent, probably has guns but no intention to use them. When serving these warrants, the unit went in carefully but cautious.

They would first cover the house, front and back, then knock on the door, announce, "King County police, we are here to serve a warrant on your marijuana grow."

When the unit was serving a tweeker, they have a device called a Gray Ghost. This is a steel pipe 5" in diameter, with ½" steel plates welded on each end. There are two handles on each side, so that two men can swing it. The pipe is 28" long.

They knocked two quick raps on the door, loudly announced that they were the police serving a warrant and the third knock was the Gray Ghost. It did not

matter if the door was locked or barred. The Ghost would take the frame with it. The officers would run in yelling with guns drawn ready for any resistance. The whole house would be secure in under sixty seconds.

About six months after the last raid the blue Camaro that was impounded along with the rest of the cars, came up for auction. Jerry was able to buy it in open auction for $800.00. He gave it to his son who was in college. His son drove it for two years, wore the tires bald, put a couple of dents in it, then sold it for $1,200.

All the police auctions are well advertised and open to the general public. Police officers were allowed to bid like any citizen with no special consideration. Jerry always attended the auctions. Sometimes a person could get something really cheap and next time the prices would be above retail. You just never knew until you were there. It was a great deal of fun to watch the people.

* * * * * * * * * * * * * *

Two of Jerry's detectives Bill and Tom had some interesting experiences. Bill, was an excellent detective, 6' 4", in his mid-30's, dark hair, always dressed well, was good looking and had a lot of charisma. He could charm a cobra. His talent was his charm. Jerry could send him to a meeting or conference and everyone he met would remember him. They liked him and still knew who he was years later. This made him very valuable to the department. Tom was 6', slim, in his early 30's, brown hair, unimpressive face, just Joe average. He had the morals of an alley cat. He never did more than he absolutely had to. Not a lot of initiative. He had previously worked for the phone company and knew how to tap into phone lines when the department was able to obtain a warrant to do so. He too, was valuable to the department, for this ability.

Bill and Tom had been watching a small time dealer in hopes of working him. Working undercover, they were driving an old beat up 2 door Sedan. They had made contact with this man and when he showed up with the dope, they had him get in the back of their car. They had to pull the back of the front seat forward to let him in. Suddenly the guy trips on them being cops. He slams the seat forward and pins Bill against the steering wheel, opens the door and bolts. They were in a downtown area and there was a lot of construction going on. Bill was in hot pursuit with Tom not far behind. The guy was running in and out and over equipment and ditches. Suddenly Tom yells out, "STOP or I'll shoot." The suspect ran around some big equipment and dove into the nearest construction ditch and was really surprised when Bill dove in right next to him. He looks at Bill hiding next to him and said "What the hell are you hiding in here for?" Bill says, "Are you shitin' me? I've seen him shoot."

The situation was defused. They made the arrest and took him to the station. Then they started working him. They convinced him that he was in big trouble, not only for dealing but for trying to evade arrest and would probably spend a lot of time in jail. They told him that if he would cooperate and worked with the police, his sentence could be held aside. If he did a good job and continued to work with them, the charges could be dropped completely. The guy finally agreed and became their informant.

A few weeks later Bill and Tom were out working street drugs. Fishing for low level hits. Tom had the flu and shouldn't have been working. He was laying down in the front seat. A guy gets in the back seat of the car and starts to negotiate the price of his drugs. - - - All of a sudden he jacks a shell in a .45 and sticks it to the back of Bill's head. "I think you guys are the fuckin' cops." Tom sits up slowly, barely opening his eyes and acts as though he is just waking up. Tom sees the gun at the back of Bills head. He says, "Wow man, cool gun. Can I see it?" Then casually takes it away from the guy.

He pretends he was just looking at it and quickly pops the round out of the chamber and empties the clip, then hands it back to the guy. "Wow man, really a cool gun!" He worked so fast that the guy didn't seem to notice what he did. They made the deal, bought the dope and the guy went on about his way. They turned in the dope as evidence and made their report. They were setting this guy up for a bigger deal and hoping to get him to turn on his dealers.

One evening Jerry and the unit were serving a warrant. They had covered the house front and back and Jerry went to the door, knocked and announced, "King County police, here to serve a warrant on your marijuana grow. The man opened the door, saw who they were and with a look of sheer terror on his face, yelled and ran back into the house. Jerry was surprised and the men entered carefully. They heard a shot and went on full alert. They began searching, guns drawn, room to room, and found the man dead. He had blown his brains out. All over a minimum charge, and he had no priors and would not even have done jail time.

When Jerry had been working narcotics for about a year his daughter Laura was born. He thought he was pretty tough but she immediately wrapped him around her little finger. Eleven months later his son Lenny was born. Jerry was very proud of all of his children and tried to spend as much time with his family as possible.

* * * * * * * * * * * * * *

An informant had reported that a doctor was dealing large quantities of excellent marijuana. So Jerry had him set up a buy for 1/2 pound. However when it came time for the delivery, it was delivered by the informant. He informed Jerry that the doctor would not deliver less than a pound. The price was $2,200.00. Meanwhile the unit began checking on the doctor and found that he had six houses in addition to his personal home and his office. He also had purchased new Porsche Turbo Carrera for each of his girlfriends. He drove a handmade Pantera that was displayed at the World's Fair and a 12 cylinder Jaguar that was remarkably fast. Each of these cars had a license plate with the doctor's name on it and a number after the name. His was a number one and two and the girls had number after that.

The informant set up a buy for a full pound. They were to meet in a parking lot. The doctor showed up and they made the buy. Strangely enough, he was the nicest guy, who was extremely proud of the quality of his marijuana. He acted as though he and Jerry were good buddies. "I tell you Jerry, my stuff is the best shit out there. It took a lot of research and good luck to get it this way. I love doing this." Jerry made several other buys from him and learned more and more about him. They discovered that he had a couple living in each of his six houses operating a highly sophisticated hydro phonic marijuana growing operation. He had also purchased cars for each of the couples in his houses. The unit found that his credit card bills for parties, dinners etc. was over $10,000 per month.

After his arrest the doctor admitted to everything and showed them a house they had missed. A regular Mr. Congeniality. Jerry thought he must have been loaded. However at his seizure hearing he was just as nice.

That night after getting all the warrants for the houses, Jerry called all the local T.V. news departments telling them who he was, asked if they would be interested in sending a news crew along when they served the warrants on the marijuana grows.

In the past, it was taboo to have any press coverage on narcotic activities at all. The stations acted as though they did not believe Jerry. Channel 14 however did want to cover it and sent a woman reporter and a cameraman. Jerry explained that they could film no license plates or detective's faces, and were not to get in the way. Otherwise they could hang close.

The reporters and cameraman went with the squad for a low key warrant. They had wired Jerry with a mike. The team served the warrant and it was a little more dramatic than normal. They knocked on the door of the first house and a man answered. The officer said "King County police. We have a search warrant for your grow operation." The man muttered something and

126

made a move toward the corner of the room where Jerry spotted 4 or 5 rifles.

Jerry quickly boomed, "Freeze or I'll blow your ass off." The man dropped to the floor and put his hands behind his head. The team quickly secured the house and a female suspect. They let the film team in and they filmed the house and the marijuana growing operation. There were about 260 plants there.

The story aired on the evening news. Suddenly all the other stations were calling and asking why they were not invited. When the folks in charge found out they were invited and did not respond Jerry was sure that some heads rolled.

The story was well accepted by the public and all the stations now wanted to climb on the band wagon. Jerry and the detective that wrote the warrants made up a press kit. It told them what they could and could not do.

They had a meeting with all the interested parties and told them they would make up a rotating list of all stations. That would allow all of them to have a equal chance to ride along when warrants were served.

Then, all hell broke loose. Most of the other departments objected to them taking the news people along. They always turned reporters down as they felt it was putting undue pressure on them. Jerry tried to explain, diplomatically, why they were doing it. Some, including the Drug Enforcement Administration understood. Jerry was able to work with them on a continuing basis. Other departments thought they were grand standing or didn't want the attention as they didn't want to work at their jobs.

At one point the top brass wanted Jerry's undercover team to let the news media take their photos. This made no sense at all. How the heck are they supposed to maintain an "undercover" presence if their faces are all over the newspapers and T.V.??

Jerry met with the top brass and explained the situation to them but they still felt that since his unit was doing so well that it was the one that should be recognized. He tried to reason with them but they had their minds set and wouldn't budge.

Jerry met with his crew and discussed plans to please the media and the brass, without giving away the entire teams identity. There would be no way to continue in their line of work with their photos all over the newspapers and T.V. They kicked several ideas around and finally decided on a plan of action. Jerry told them to be ready when the reporters came and they were.

Finally Jerry had to let the reporters in. He told his team to each grab anything they could find for a disguise and be ready to be photographed. Well, when they all showed up with faces drawn on paper bags over their heads, the news people got such a kick out of it that they went ahead and ran the story with that photo.

*   *   *   *   *   *   *   *   *   *   *   *   *   *

As this case is very sensitive we will call the city Watatchkee. As part of an ongoing investigation, Jerry and one of his men John arrested a woman who tried to sell drugs to them. She was a beautiful woman and used her beauty as a tool. To reduce the charges against herself she agreed to lead them to some major dealers. She claimed that a judge and the prosecuting attorney of that city where doing a huge business. They couldn't work out of their county so they got hold of their Sheriff who in turn contacted the Executive Director of that county who called the Governor. The Governor got back to them two hours later and said it sounded like a good deal and to go for it.

They drove to that county with the woman in the car. When they got there and fitted her with a wire, they had her call the prosecuting attorney, tell him she was back in town and that she wanted to get some shit. She also called the judge and told him the same thing. The attorney, Ron, took her out to dinner. She asked him to get her three kilos of coke to take back to Seattle. During dinner they both snorted coke and he took her back to his apartment. He wanted oral sex and she went in to the bathroom and removed the wire and put it in her purse. She was supposed to leave it on the whole time but she thought she could not, when naked. Jerry and Bob still had all the rest of the evening recorded. Afterwards she put it back on and asked him if she could pay for two kilos now and pay for the third in a week. He said he didn't know and would have to check with the judge, Todd.

The next night she met Todd and the same thing happened. Again she was wearing the wire and Jerry and John taped the whole thing.

Two hours later she called Todd and asked if he had okayed her request about the extra kilo of coke. He said he would but she would have to "do" him extra for it. She wore the wire again, and the evening was taped again. The next day she called Ron and asked if she was going to get the shit and he agreed to meet her in a parking lot. When they got there the parking lot was a solid sheet of ice. The woman could hardly stand up to get to Ron's car, even with her boots on. This time she was wearing a wire and a beeper. As soon as she saw the coke she was to hit the button on the beeper and Jerry and John and their team would pick up the signal and rush there.

They were positioned concealed around the outside of the parking lot. She was only there about 30 seconds when she pushed the button. The team spilled out of their cars, slipping and sliding all around the lot trying to hurry and looking like the Keystone cops. Two of their guys had a brand new Monte Carlo under cover car. They came on to the lot about 10 mph and tried to stop. The car was all over the place. They couldn't steer, tried the brakes with no luck, even put it in reverse and went sailing on by Jerry and his men at 10 miles per hour. The whole thing was like one big cartoon.

Ron was wondering what all these crazy guys were doing, falling all over and coming toward him. He was so busy laughing at them he didn't even realize they were coming for him.

They were dressed in blue wind breakers with "Sheriff Department" on the back and "Police" on the front. They also had blue baseball caps with "Police" on them. When they were close enough for him to be able to read their emblems he knew who they were but still did not know they were after him until they stuck a gun in the window and read him his rights. He was put in one car and Jerry and John and another officer went in to town to the judge's corporate office.

When they got there they found out that Todd was in chambers. Jerry walked back and opened the door. The secretary asked "Who are you?" Jerry showed her his badge and said "We are here to bust your boss. Any shit from you and you go to jail too." The other two stayed with her and Jerry burst into the judge's chambers. The judge looked up from what he was reading, startled and said "Who the hell are you?" "I'm the guy who is going to ruin your day." "Get the hell out of my office." "Excuse me your honor... Oh, excuse me again, it's not your honor any more. It's come with me maggot, you're under arrest," he said as he was pulling out his badge.

They went to the local Sheriff's office with both Ron and Todd hand cuffed in the back of a car. They asked to call their Sheriff and to put it on a conference call. The secretary said she couldn't but could put it on speaker phone, was that all right? Jerry also asked them to tape the call. He thought it was a good idea.

When their Sheriff came on the line, he said "Hi Jerry I guess this call is because you have something to report. The local Sheriff perked up at that. Jerry went on to explain the whole story. At first they thought the local Sheriff was going to give them trouble but as more info. was revealed, he began to smile. When he got to the part that both men were under arrest and outside cuffed in the parking lot, he actually cracked up laughing. He said "You don't know how happy I am to hear that. I have suspected as much for the last couple of years but didn't have enough to go after them. He was then extremely happy to assist them in any way he could.

With these arrests his department was able to track down the rest of their organization and made several more arrests. That Sheriff went to his head honcho and they hired two Federal Prosecutors from California to handle the case.

* * * * * * * * * * * * * *

When local police were required to work with federal agencies, there were often problems. The federal agencies called the police, "local yokels" and the police called the FBI "Fuckin' Bunch of Idiots", etc. However, Jerry had developed a friendship with two agents from the FBI as he worked with them to teach them his team's highly successful undercover techniques. He also spent time going to Canada to teach classes to the RCMP about outlaw motorcycle gangs, during the same time period.

Jerry's team had an IRS agent, who was the wife of a car dealer who rented staff undercover cars to the county. She was another agent they could work with.

There was a radical group called "George Jackson Brigade". In today's era they would have been called terrorists. They robbed banks for income and were

"Hate Mongers." They robbed a bank in Belleview and shot a police officer. This got everyone's attention. Not only did the Feds get involved, but every other agency as well. The gang consisted of five males and four females. One of the leaders was a woman named Rita Brown. She had a Brindle Great Dane she loved that went everywhere with her. The team got a tip that she used a laundry matt at Richmond beach to wash her clothes. This was a very exclusive area. Jerry discussed the case with the FBI and they decided to conduct a joint surveillance at the laundry matt. They had a small semi they parked in front of the mall, with mall advertising on it.

Jerry and Bill with two FBI agents were part of the two teams that worked each shift of the surveillance. They maintained it for two and a half weeks. Talk about boring. At the end of that period the FBI commander said that he would have to pull his team as he could no longer justify the man power. He intended to pull them at the end of the present shift. Jerry's sergeant said that he had a feeling that something would happen and he decided to maintain it for one more week.

Three days later, at eleven p.m., an old beat up car pulled up and parked in front of the laundry. A woman got out and took a load of laundry in. Her hair, age and facial features did not look like the photos of Rita at all. They continued watching, even though they were pretty sure it was not Rita. After all, what else was there to do? About twenty minutes after she entered, a head popped out the back seat window of the car.

It was a Brindle Great Dane!   They had a basket of clothes in the semi to take in, if they needed a closer look so Bill took it in for a look.   If he decided it was her, he was to run his fingers through his hair to let them know. He didn't even take time to put any money in the washer when he was running his fingers through his hair over and over.   She must have thought he had really bad dandruff.

The team exited the semi from the back and worked their way, while concealed, to the laundry matt, then rushed in and jumped her.   She did not resist.   She had rubber face make up that was not well done and had died her hair.

Jerry got on the phone to his boss and had him call the FBI hot line.   He said "Do not put anything over the air.   These people are listening in."   It took Jerry's Sergeant and the FBI almost an hour to get there.   Rita was not talking.   She just kept saying, "Fuck you."   They ran the plates on the car and found it was stolen.   They had no clue where the gangs headquarters were.   Then Jerry came up with an idea.   He called the Animal Control department and had them run the dogs license tags.   It was twelve p.m. by now but he got an answer and an address.   It turned out it was two blocks away from Jerry's house.   That was a pretty scary feeling.

The FBI commander complemented Jerry on the idea.   The FBI got their SWAT team ready to go.   It was about twelve miles from the laundry matt. Then, for some unknown reason, the FBI officer in charge got on the radio to the FBI com center and told them where they were going. Jerry's boss heard him talking and ran over and yelled, "For Christ sakes did you put that over the air?"   The FBI man said "Well yea."   Jerry's boss yelled "Lets go now."   They burned rubber roaring out of the parking lot with the FBI team scrambling for their cars to follow.   Jerry's team hit the house in five minutes and "stuffed" the door. They rushed in hot and heavy.

There was a complete radio command center, picking up all frequencies from King County, Seattle and the FBI. There was hot coffee in cups on the table, warm bowels of soup on the stove, burning cigarettes in the ash trays, but everyone was gone.

They found huge stacks of radio logs with details of every single radio transmission, the amount of time it took officers to respond, which officers were efficient and which were slow or not as organized. It was scary how much information they were able to compile from radio calls and how accurate it was.

They had missed this gang by seconds and it took another six months to catch them. Then it was only because the gang themselves made a big mistake.

* * * * * * * * * * * * * *

Ten months after Jerry took over the Narcotic department, he was pleased to hear that the law that he, Dave and the financial executive had worked to change was passed. Due to the work he did encouraging the news media to cover drug related arrests, they got the publicity they needed. With the new funds available to the agency they were able to fund the DARE program, hire additional staff and buy desperately needed equipment. Jerry was extremely proud of this accomplishment. It had taken a lot of work, planning, preparation and luck to make it happen.

Jerry worked for two and a half years as the head of the Narcotic department. They set every record in King County for number of arrests, quantity of drugs seized and value of property seized. They had served 228 warrants the first year and continued to do well from then on. Jerry had his own car lot. They had well over 100 cars in an isolated county impound lot that were seized in drug deliveries. Some of the cars were used for undercover work, some sent to other police departments. The rest were sold at public auction. It was really a pain in the ass, trying to keep records straight and everything on the up and up.

* * * * * * * * * * * * * *

It was mid-summer and Jerry found a weekend that had nothing on the calendar. He told the team, "No deals this weekend I have a crew coming to paint my house. Put calls off until Monday." At 6:00am on Sunday he got a call from the Auto Theft Detective who said that he got a call from a very reliable informant that two guys just rolled into town with two kilos of heroin. That amount was almost unheard of. They were looking to move it right away. Jerry was wrestling with himself while the detective was talking. He really needed to stay home that weekend. He told him to go ahead and set up a time to meet and let him know.

As soon as the Auto Theft Detective Bill, called him back with the meeting time and location Jerry paged his team. With the new pagers they all had, he just typed in a code number and they all knew to call ASAP. The whole team agreed to go. Bill wanted to be in on it, so with eight of Jerry's team they would stake out the meet area and see what happened. Bill had his informant call the seller and asked if he could give a potential buyer his phone number and the guy said OK. George, Jerry's senior guy, was to pose as a buyer. Jerry still did not really believe the whole thing. Dopers were not very reliable.

George called the seller and arranged to meet him at McDonald's on the east side of King County for a sample to be tested. When they got there George was only in there about five minutes and came right back out. They gave him a whole gram and didn't charge him for anything. This was unheard of. This was one weird deal. That was $300.00 worth of heroin. The all drove away and got out of the area. To test the drug they had small tubes similar to glow stick tubes. They would put a pinch of dope in the tube, break the vile inside and if it turned purple it was real. Well, they dropped a flake in and broke the vile and it instantly turned a bright purple. They had never seen anything turn that quick or so bright.

George called back and negotiated a price for the whole two kilos. The seller finally agreed to $35,000 per kilo, but said the price would be higher the next time. George agreed but said that since it was Sunday the most he could get his hands on was $40,000 but if the seller would front him the dope he would have the rest Monday night. The seller agreed.

When anyone does a dope deal, you "trip" (move from spot to spot, looking for surveillance or anything out of order). Jerry thought that this deal would have to trip three to five more times at least. The seller said he wanted to meet them at the Safeway parking lot in Renton in an hour and a half and George agreed. Jerry's team got there way ahead of time and he positioned four of his team around the parking lot just moving slowly around as though they were customers. Bill and Jerry went over to the gas station in the middle of the parking lot where they had a excellent view of the whole area and after showing the manager their badges told him that they needed to pretend that they worked there so that they could do some surveillance work for a short time. The man agreed but said "Ok, just don't get me shot at." "Well, better you than me." he went white, but then Jerry laughed. "Oh, ok." then he laughed nervously.

A short time later they saw a nice looking black Ford pickup with Mexican license plates, a young Mexican driving and the white guy George met before, beside him. George was in the middle of the parking lot and they drove up to him. The truck stopped and the white guy got out with a large bag and went to meet George and the kid drove over to the gas station and started to fill the truck up. There were several cases of soda on the floor in the office so Bill and Jerry started moving them from side to side so it would look like they were working there.

Just then the pager went off, that met the dope was there. Jerry shoved his gun in the Mexican's face and said "You're under arrest." Suddenly a Renton police squad car came screaming into the lot, tires smoking and the man jumped out with his gun drawn yelling, "FREEZE, drop your guns!" Jerry held up his badge and yelled back, "King county narcotics! we're working, we're working." The cop said "Got any more guys here?" "Yea, a squad over by Safeway making an arrest." The local cop got on the radio and told his men what was going on. Jerry's team arrested both men and got all the heroin. Then they had to visit the Renton shift commander.

They found out that the Safeway had recently been robbed. It seemed an employee had noticed Jerry's men hanging around. One of the officers bent over and when he did, an employee in the store saw his gun. The employee called it in and several of them were screaming and headed for the back door.

Jerry had to kiss ass. He knew that when you were going to work in another agencies jurisdiction you were supposed to let them know. He explained that he didn't know it was going down there. They thought that it would just be another stop on the "Trip". They also had to apologize to the people at Safeway as well. After all these guys were in plain clothes and did not look like Police. They wrapped everything up and took the men downtown. No one was used to seeing that much heroin.

They found out that the young Mexican was the white man's son-in-law. It seems the older man owned a mine in Mexico and had traveled across the border for the past 25 years. The border guards knew him and since his daughter married a Mexican everyone on both sides liked him. At one point he had a small box built secretly under the floor boards of his truck. He was smuggling gold from his mine across the border on a regular basis as he got more money in the U.S. Then someone got the bright idea that instead of getting $600.00 an ounce for Gold, he could smuggle Heroin for $3,500 an ounce. The kid went out and bought two kilos of Heroin put it in the box and drove across the border.

Jerry's team had torn the truck apart and along with other evidence found a receipt for several nights in a motel room in San Francisco. While there they were running out of money, so the Mexican went out and bought a "$100 paper" of Heroin to see how big it was and how it was packaged. They were not users and had no idea that it was cut, "stepped on" to about 20% of the original strength. Their Heroin was 90%. They were cutting off small chunks and sealing with box tape into $100 size packages and then went out and sold several packages on the street.

Jerry called San Francisco narcotic and asked it they had any unusual Heroin events during those nights. It seems that they had nineteen ODs that required hospitalization and seven of them died.

If you kill someone while in commission of a felony it is murder. The men were convicted and sent to prison. Jerry's team impounded the truck.

* * * * * * * * * * * * * *

One afternoon an informant contacted one of Jerry's men and told him that there were two guys from California who wanted to sell multiple kilos of coke. They wanted "Flash Money." (seeing the money up front) before showing the drugs. They were looking for $150,000.00. Jerry's budget did not have that available so he contacted DEA and asked if they wanted in. They did. Six of their team arrived and they partnered a female agent with Jerry's best, George.

The pushers had instructed the "buyers," to rent a motel room in Belleview and they would get hold of them. Jerry rented the room right away and had it wired and video cameras installed. The pushers called and set a time to meet. They were both driving Porsches. George and the female DEA agent arrived in a Corvette. They met the pushers in the room but the pushers kept referring to the coke as "cream". Jerry was really proud of his agent as he said "When you deliver the cocaine, I mean cream." The pusher blurted out, "Damn it, don't say that word. We want to see the money first."

George showed him the case with $150,000.00 and said he wanted seven kilos. The pusher said "No way the minimum amount we will take is $35,000 a key. I can move it anywhere for that. This is top grade stuff and not cut." They started to leave and said "We will call you." After three hours the DEA agent said he would have to call his people off as he couldn't justify the overtime. The female agent who had worked with Jerry's team in the past asked if she could stay on. He agreed providing Jerry would be responsible for her. He agreed.

An hour later the pushers called and said that they would meet at a big hotel in the University district. The DEA agent called her boss and told him they were "tripping". Jerry called their prosecutor and said it was going down quickly and they wanted him there. He said that they were going to need several search warrants. He was going to the judge to get them signed. It was one thirty a.m. He said Jerry could call him from the Hotel so he could write and sign them right away.

They got to the hotel, walked into the lobby and one of the pushers was waiting with a little metal suit case. He sees George and the DEA agent and walks back outside with them to their Corvette. Everyone outside is scrambling to get close enough but stay out of sight. The pusher throws the suit case on top of the Corvette, pops it open and shows the four and a half kilo of coke and says, "Where's the money?" The DEA agent reaches into the Corvette and grabs an empty case and George grabs the guy and face plants him on the Corvette and says, "Police, you're under arrest." The team responds and as soon as he is hand cuffed, a big car pulls into the driveway. The team thinks it is the other pusher and runs over with guns drawn. It turns out it is the prosecutor and the judge.

The judge says, "I wanted to come, just once and not miss all the excitement. I don't get to see things happen. I only get involved long after it's all done." They all went into the hotel breakfast area, as they had no idea where the second pusher was. When they searched the man they arrested they found a hotel key to room 815. They started going over the hotel records but couldn't get any further information. Just then the elevator door opened and there was the second pusher. He saw several people behind the counter, but no guns or badges so he just walked outside. He was only carrying a small shaving kit.

Jerry and two men fell in behind him, like a small parade. He keeps looking back expecting them to say something. They follow him to his Porsche and as he reaches for the door Jerry says "Hold it buddy, we want to talk to you. Narcotic unit, King County. What's in the bag?" He handed Jerry the bag, there was $35,000.00 in cash in it. "Who does this belong to, and where are you going this time of night?" As quickly as he answered Jerry would fire another question at him. They were trying to keep him from leaving because as of this moment they did not have "probable cause" to arrest him. "Whose car is this? Where do you live? What is your mother's name? Are you staying at this hotel?" and on and on. After three or four minutes one of Jerry's men poked his head out of the hotel and said "We have probable cause!"

They spun him around and cuffed him and read him

his rights. He clammed up immediately. They took him back inside the hotel and sat the two of them down together. They got the prosecutor into the room and explained the situation.   He wrote the search warrants for both Porsches and the motel room. They went to the room and found four big metal suit cases. The first one had six kilos of coke, the second had six kilos of coke, the third had six kilos of coke and the fourth, the heaviest of all, was packed so full of money, even one more dollar would not have fit.

They took the prisoners, the coke and the money back to their office and jail in the court house and the Porsches to the garage where they were given a brief search.

Jerry and three others counted the money. They would take one stack at a time and first one man would count it, write down his total then pass it to the next. He would do the same and pass it to the third and so forth. If there were any discrepancies they would have to count that stack again. It took them several hours and the final count was $158,750.00. Then they needed to fill out "seizure forms" for the money, the coke and the cars. It was now ten a.m. the next morning and they were beat.

When the judge looked at the final report he said "This is some outstanding police work." They were just getting ready to go home and the DEA supervisor showed up. He congratulated them for sticking it out. He was very nice and friendly. He came up to Jerry and said "I am catching shit for leaving too soon. Can we share in the press release and the money?" Jerry answered "Sure, no problem." So they went to the evidence room and Jerry signed the money over to him. He took it, shook Jerry's hand and said "Great work and thanks a lot."

A week and a half later the DEA supervisor called and said "Can I come and see you?" He shows up with a metal suit case and informs Jerry that there is a law that once a state agency seizes something a Federal agency could not re-seize it. So he gave it all back.

The case went to Federal court, because of the quantity and Jerry testified. Both men were found guilty of all charges. The Federal judge, in open court room said "This was some of the best police work I have ever seen and I wish that the Federal agency's could bring in cases like this." That was a wonderful feather in the teams cap.

A short time later the pushers attorneys called and stated that his client said that the older Porsche was a collector's item and wanted to buy it back for $35,000.00. Jerry was suspicious and decided to check on it before giving him an answer. He called a couple of Porsche dealers to find out what it would be worth and the highest appraisal was $20,000. Something was definitely wrong. He searched the car again and found nothing then decided to call the "customs" agency and ask them to bring a drug dog over. They took the seats out and had the dog go through the car. He hit "big time" on the back floor boards and behind the seat.

The mechanics had some impact metal cutters and they cut out the interior body and found secret compartments with three kilos of coke and a nine m.m. pistol. Then they had the dog go over it one more time, but found nothing more. They threw the seats and the scrap metal back into the car. Since it had tinted windows you couldn't see what was inside. They Jerry called their attorney and said "Sure, we'll sell it to you."

The attorney shows up with a check for $35,000.00. Jerry will only accept cash. The attorney is really pissed but leaves then comes back with the cash. Jerry does all the paper work then hands him the keys. Meanwhile all the mechanics are trying really hard not to laugh as they know what is coming.

The attorney goes to the Porsche, opens the door and sees what is inside and goes ballistic. The head mechanic says, "Buddy you own it now and you've got two hours to get that out of here or it goes back into impound." The attorney called a tow truck and towed it off. The next day he raised hell with the county attorney, who said "Well, sometimes you get to do the fuckin' and sometimes you get fucked"

* * * * * * * * * * * * * *

Jerry and his team soon learned that the Sheriff was going to retire. They were not looking forward to someone new. It would be hard for anyone to do as good a job as their present Sheriff. They all doubted anyone else would be as well liked either.

As it turned out their apprehensions were well founded. It seems as though they would be getting someone that none of his previous crew liked, much less respected.

When the sheriff quit, he was replaced by a new sheriff from Idaho. Samuels was 6'2" a pudgy 270 lbs., round face and looked like he had been eating milk toast all his life. He wore every piece of gold, silver or ribbon he could find. He looked like a Mexican general.

He came from a department of 190 people to this department of over 1,000 and didn't know what he was doing. This guy thought he could completely disregard the department's policy. You do not take or except gratuity. The department felt very strongly about that. The first thing he did was to attend a Sea Hawks game in full uniform, with his family, expecting to get in free. It was a huge embarrassment to police officers in general and to the entire department. It was all over the area in a couple of hours. When Jerry heard this man was their next sheriff he called the Idaho Police department. Jerry said "Well, it looks like we are getting him, what can you tell me about him?" They just laughed and said "Thank God you are getting him. We are finally getting rid of him."

Everyone was complaining about the new Sheriff and how he was trying to control each department. He was not even beginning to honor the code of ethics that the department had always been known for. It seemed as though all he wanted to do was put his time in until he retired and not make any attempt to handle the crime situation.

Several officers could not help but wonder if he was on the take. It just seemed as though he would look the other way in many cases. It was really a disappointment for the men that had been working so hard to make a difference.

A lot of the officers felt like giving up completely. It was very discouraging.

The new sheriff wanted narcotics to sit on their asses and do only little street dealers.

He ordered them to stay low key and don't make any waves. Jerry said "Bull Shit" We are doing an ass kicking job and I intend to keep doing it." The sheriff said "You won't do that if you keep working for me!" Jerry said "What's the problem? Would that hurt your income?"

The sheriff's face turned beet red, "You can't talk to me that way." Jerry shot back, "Fuck you! How's that for talking back?" The sheriff said "Pack your bags, cause you're outa here!" Jerry replied "I knew about you ahead of time. My bags have been packed for a week! Oh and by the way, you might want to read the article that just came out in the Seattle Post - Intelligencer;

Then you can figure out what excuse to give to the public when they want to know why the department is no longer fighting the drug war."

144

KING COUNTY POLCE
Near record in the value of narcotics seized

" The value of narcotics seized so far this year by King County narcotics detectives is approaching record levels. Through October, the county's corps of narcs had seized slightly more than $5 million worth of cocaine in drug raids. That compares with about $445,000 worth seized in all of 1986.

Seizures of black tar heroin, too, have skyrocketed from just over $104,000 in 1968 to more than $1.7 million through October of this year, county statistics show.

At the same time, however, the total value of marijuana taken has fallen from more than $3 million last year to nearly $6000,000 through October this year.

But with more than a month to go drug seizure value still have more than doubled from just over $3 million in 1986 to about $7.3 million through last month.

That nearly matches the record in 1985 when more than $7.8 million worth of drugs were confiscated, including $4.2 in black tar heroin and $2.2 million in cocaine.

Price does not account for the dollar differences. In fact, police said because of dealer competition, cocaine now sells for a little as $60 a gram on the street, compared with $125 a year ago. Prices of black tar heroin and marijuana also have dropped.

The increases over 1986 also doesn't necessarily mean there are more drugs in the county. Sgt. Jerry Jorgenson, head of the narcotics unit said the county now has a bigger enforcement team.

Last year, Jorgenson had seven detectives but functioned with an average of four throughout the year because three were farmed out to various police task forces.

This year, the unit was beefed up to 11 detectives and a sergeant was added.

The cocaine seized was "fake" or powdered cocaine, Jorgenson said. He said unincorporated King County hasn't seen as much crack, or rock, cocaine, an inexpensive, pure derivative that is plaguing Seattle's poorer neighborhoods.

The biggest cocaine haul was June 6th when 34 pounds were seized in a South King County residence, according to Jorgenson.

Black tar heroin is almost exclusively a product of Mexico, often smuggled into the United States by illegal aliens, police said.

Cocaine, on the other hand, finds it's way here by a variety of means. That manufactured in California, authorities say, arrives by sea and air smuggling routes, often in Florida and California.

Marijuana seizure are down because so many cocaine and heroin cases have popped up and occupied detectives time."

Jerry went back to work as a patrol shift supervisor and was required to inspect every body that was found, to determine if the cause of death was a crime, an accident or natural causes. He had from seventeen to thirty officers working under him per shift. He pushed hard for a good solid program that would turn out well qualified officers and insisted they toe the line. There were times when there was just no way a candidate was going to make it.

This was a problem as when affirmative action was implanted the candidate would cry "discrimination". They could say they were fired because they were, black, Mexican, a woman or that he just didn't like them. Jerry got very good at getting them to quit. He would take them aside and explain to them that in spite of their best efforts there was just no way they could make it. If he had to fire them then when they tried to get another job he would have to tell the new perspective employer that they had been fired and why. If, however they quit, all he had to tell them was that yes they had worked there and had quit.

He worked in this capacity for a year and a half until he could retire.

* * * * * * * * * * * * * * *

Chapter 6
Moving, Movies and FEMA

After Jerry retired he went to work for a "pull tab" company. He did very well and within a year he was the vice president. He had 64 people working for him, printing, numbering, laminating and packaging. He was in charge of buying materials and shipping as well. That business really took off.

Their customers were, truck stops, restaurants, bars, night clubs, gambling halls, Bingo halls, bowling alleys and dance halls. It exploded in the mid-west.

The big bingo houses picked it up and bought the entire packages. Jerry had his people running like a well-oiled machine. They were turning out the finished product and keeping up with the demand. Things seemed to be going well, but then the owner seemed to begin to make some really bad decisions. He appeared unstable. It was as though he was constantly in a crises mode.

He pulled his best salesman out of the mid-west.. The customers there were buying because they liked and respected him. It seems the boss developed a father faddish toward the young man and wanted him closer to him. Then he replaced him with a guy with mental problems and sales collapsed by 50%.

Now they had too many workers and were way over stocked with product. Jerry was miffed as he had worked hard to make that happen and now they were losing business.

Jerry went in to talk to the boss and they had a big disagreement. The boss told him that he was getting a loan to re-equip and re-establish sales. Jerry knew he couldn't get a loan in the conventional way and pressed to find out where he was going to get it. He was leery of the company the boss planned to deal with so he got one of his friends from the police department to check on the company for him. It turned out it was tied to organized crime. They had been trying to get into the pull tab business for some time. Jerry went back and explained it to his boss and said that he didn't want any part of it. The boss said that he could leave whenever he wanted to. Jerry pointed out that he had made him an officer of the corporation that he would have to buy him out. They then agreed on a price and he did buy Jerry out.

Jerry and his wife decided they would move and she said that she wanted to move to Kelso, Washington near her family. They packed up their 5th wheel and went to Kelso and parked in a trailer park. She was going to stay there and look for a place and a job. Meantime Jerry stayed in Seattle with the kids and took care of their house there. He and the kids would head down there each weekend to see what she found. She worked as a loan officer at a bank and should have been able to find something right away. After eight weeks, while she had found a few places she was interested in buying she hadn't even tried to find a job. When Jerry asked her what the heck was going on she started crying and said she didn't want to live there, she hated it and did not want to live that close to her family. Jerry packed everything back up in the 5th wheel and they went back to Seattle.

Jerry and his brother Fred decided to tour north Idaho looking for a location. Jerry had a "collage theses" going for all of north Idaho. It included info. on mortgage rates, power, water, insurance, crime rates and so forth. The cheapest place was Idaho County and Grangeville. It had great building laws and was the most independent. Jerry found a place and put a down payment on a 3400 sq. ft. home on 84 acres. He went home, put their house up for sale and sold it 4 times. The 4th time it finally went through. He loaded up the family and went to look at the place in Grangeville. Just half way there his wife started complaining before she even saw it. "I don't like it, it is too remote." and was griping all the way. Jerry said "Fuck it that is where we are going to live." When they got there she said it was a nice house but it was too far out and she didn't want to live there. They didn't talk all the way back to Washington.

As they were packing the house Lenny got sick. They thought it was the flu but it seemed worse so they took him to the doctor. It seems he had type I Diabetes. -

Jerry called the real estate agent and asked if the hospital there had facilities to treat Diabetes. The realtor said his wife was a nurse there and he would find out. When the agent called back he said there were no facilities there in that small hospital. Jerry was impressed with his honesty as this deal was a financial loss for him, but he helped them get out of the deal and everyone involved understood.

Jerry and his wife were able to get a book of homes for sale and found a beautiful Victorian home in Wallace, Idaho. They loaded up their 5th wheel and went to the Silver Valley to look at it. When they got there and saw it they decided that there was just too much work that needed to be done. The real estate agent that showed them the house said that he had heard about another place that the owner was thinking about selling but was not yet on the market. It was on Cedar St. nearby so they drove by and really liked it. Four hours later he was able to make an appointment for them to see it. Jerry's wife loved it and they bought it.

He told the owners that he wanted to move in, in two weeks. The owners were surprised that it would close that soon but said ok.

Jerry went hunting while they were waiting, but when it came time to move, the six people who said they would help, didn't show up. He rented two trucks and together with his truck and trailer and the help of the kids, his wife, older son Perry and his wife, Anglia, they got everything loaded from the storage shed and headed to Wallace. When they were pulling into town they drove by the high school and Jerry saw the football team practicing in the field. He pulled over and went to talk to the coach. He told him that he wanted to hire the defensive line to help unload the trucks and he would pay them $7.00 per hour each, with a 5 hour minimum. Six of them showed up at nine a.m. Saturday morning and with Perry in the truck, Jerry's wife at the front door, Anglia and Laura in the house pointing to where they wanted things, he and Perry moving things as well. They got it done. Jerry was really impressed with the boys. They were hard workers, not even taking a break. They were polite, efficient, wore their hats on frontward and their pants where they belonged. Jerry knew he was home.

They had moved there in October and in the following spring, the area was hit by a massive flood. Jerry volunteered to help people get clear then helped clean up their flooded homes. He had been doing this for several days when a FEMA employee approached him and said that he had spoken to several people and knew Jerry's background and wanted to know if he would want to work for them. Jerry thought it was a volunteer position and said "Sure I could do that." It involved carrying sensitive documents for small business administration to aid flood victims. There was a lot of personal information as well as social security numbers in the paper work and required a government employee to transport them. He was to transport them on a daily basis from all the areas affected by the flooding. He was surprised to find out that it was a paid position.

He would leave home at 5:00am six days a week, drive the FEMA van to Coeur D'Alene, Kellogg, St. Maries, Orofino, Lapwai, Lewiston, Moscow and back to Coeur D'Alene. He would get home between 7:00pm and 8:00p.m. To begin with, he was driving a FEMA van, but Jerry noticed that some of the "good ol' boys" in the country did not like anything government. He warned the FEMA people that there might be trouble but they did not listen to him until a logging truck ran him off the road. They finally agreed to get him a different rig and he ended up with a Ford Explorer.

It was 1997 and during this time a Hollywood film crew came to Wallace to make a movie, "Dante's Peak". They changed the look of the whole town, adding signs and fake store fronts. At one point they covered the whole town with shredded paper for the volcano ash. They rebuilt and repaired several areas to the delight of the town folks.

Someone had rented a house next to Jerry's family. When Jerry would leave early in the morning their dog would come out and bark and he was concerned that the barking would wake the whole neighborhood. One evening he decided to go introduce himself to the new people and see if he could get an introduction to the dog so that he would not bark at him so much. A very nice lady came to the door who was staying there alone and he introduced himself and met her dog. After a short visit

150

she said "Oh, you are the neighbor that is always cooking that wonderful smelling food over there all the time." Jerry agreed and invited her to come over that evening and eat with them.

When he went back to the house his wife was all excited and said "Do you know who that is?" He said no, and she said "That's Linda Hammons." Jerry said "Who's that?"

That evening Linda joined them and went on and on about how good the food was. She said that she was always on a diet and never had anything good. Then she told Jerry that if she swiped something off his plate, the calories wouldn't count. She began coming over to eat on a regular basis and got to be friends with the family. Meanwhile the FEMA job was coming to an end and they approached him and wanted to sign Jerry up to work for them permanently as a disasters assistant officer. He agreed and they signed him up but he was not assigned a job right away.

When Jerry told Linda that the FEMA job was coming to an end, she told him she wanted to hire him as her body guard. Jerry didn't think she had anyone to be afraid of, but she said the film company would let her hire him and would pay him well. She hired him and he drove her everywhere she wanted to go. On her days off she would go to Coeur d'Alene. She would dress down with no make-up and no one recognized her. They got to be good friends and later after she went back to Hollywood and she got married she invited him to her wedding.

*   *   *   *   *   *   *   *   *   *   *   *   *   *

The movie crew was still wrapping up in Wallace when Jerry got his next FEMA assignment. Several small towns near Boise, Idaho were almost totally destroyed by mud slides. One remote town had been built on an "Alluvial fan." This is a fan or cone shaped deposit of sediment caused by and built up by streams. Usually a wide area directly below a narrow river valley.

The fan is built up by debris. Then over a period it of time, brush, mud, grasses and up rooted trees collect there. Later dirt and soil is laid down on top of it.

The town had been there for some time and had not experienced mud slides. Over the years dirt had been collecting in brush and debris above in the valley. It built up around the river that ran from the upper narrow valley and down near the town. There had been excessive amounts of heavy rain fall that spring over a long period of time. The valley floor became saturated and everything gave way. All that water and the saturated built up debris and mud slid down, flooding the wide valley floor and destroying most of the town there.

The motel and several other buildings ended up in the river. Only the trailer park was spared.

Jerry was to report to the Disaster Field Office, (DFO) in Boise. Marty Potter was the assistant director assigned to region 10. He had been overly impressed with Jerry's work in wrapping up the previous assignment taking all the small business loans and grants around, and had everything so well organized that when he and his assistants got there to close the event out, they had nothing to do and got to play golf. He and Jerry really hit it off and he was responsible for signing Jerry on and getting him to Boise to help.

As a district employee, with his card and badge, he was assigned to logistics. When Jerry arrived, Marty said "Hi Jerry, you're going to be my security man." Jerry said he wasn't interested in security and Marty said "Tough shit, you're my security man." Then he fired off a memo to Washington D.C. saying "Don't send a security person. I already have my own." Now, almost anyone else in Washington D.C. would have rammed that answer down his throat, but Marty had so much seniority and power they let him have his way. He was bringing their memos back to Jerry and laughing his ass off. He was having a great time. Now, like it or not, Jerry was Chief Head of Security for the DFO.

Jerry was using a very expensive badge machine to make the necessary badges for the local security people he hired. It cost about $5,500.00. Then he had to have security around and in the building 24 hours a day as in the complex there were a number of offices and services that all required government security. They had the same security as a court house or Federal building. There was the Small Business Administration, The Corps of Engineers, The Disaster Awareness Office, The Inspector's Office, The Appraiser's Office, and The Maps and Property Ownership Dept. They had a machine that would print maps seven feet long, worth several thousand dollars. Then there were all the materials and supplies that had to be protected so that they couldn't be stolen to create counterfeit material.

At one point the women that were working there had their change that they kept in the small containers on the top of their desks, disappearing. At first they thought someone had just borrowed it and would repay it the next day. Then everyone was hit and it was amounting to quite a bit. They talked to Jerry about it and he set up two desks, next to each other then stood outside and watched the janitorial staff that night. Sure enough it was one of the young men who was going desk to desk searching for money and taking what he found.

Jerry caught him red handed and told him to leave and he was not to come back into the building, ever. He then reported it to the head of the janitorial staff.

One of the business owners in one small town was causing trouble at the community meetings. He was disrupting the meeting demanding way more than the appraised value of his business trying to claim the loss of personal property. He should have had his own personal insurance. He was very angry and threatening the FEMA employees. He did not think they were giving him enough money. Marty asked Jerry to go to the next meeting in case there was trouble. All Jerry did was stand quietly up at the front, and everything went smoothly.

Afterwards, the man came up to him and said "I know why you are here and you handled it very well." The man did not cause any more trouble.

On the way back to the DFO Marty lost his two way radio and was very upset about it. He was really happy when Jerry re-traced their footsteps and found it where he left it at a service station. It was a $2,500.00 radio.

As the event shut down, Rick Elder, the head of all of FEMA security, in Washington D.C., called Jerry and told him they wanted him to come and work for them. He said they were having a class in May and would like him to come and be certified and become one of the "cadre". There were only 68 to cover the entire U.S. and the territories. Jerry said he didn't really want to work security. Rick said that as long as he was in region 10, Marty Porter would have him working security. He then said "I don't know what they are paying you now, but here is what I will pay you." Jerry was surprised, it was triple the amount he was getting. Jerry said "Send me the info. I will be there."

He went. It was at a highly classified place in Virginia.

* * * * * * * * * * * * * *

154

Jerry's next assignment was the island of Guam. A typhoon had destroyed most of the buildings and FEMA was going there to help.

Guam is a long narrow island approximately 40 miles by 8 miles. There are eighteen villages that include the biggest city. It has the biggest K mart in the world. They even have tour bus that takes folks to K mart. All the power was out and the poles were down. Most of stores and the big resort and big fancy hotels had their own generators. Guam had become the tourist destination for Japan.

The condo that Jerry and the FEMA team stayed in was new and units were selling for $1.2 million. The building was an elaborate, 32 stories high structure, had a huge pool, weight room, gym, a small theater, great view on a hill, small food and drug stores in the basement and just 1/4 of mile from the beach. They also had their own generator, but it wasn't putting out enough power for them to be able to open all the rooms. FEMA and The Red Cross teams were taking most of the rooms.

Gibson Electric from California had their trucks shipped over and brought concrete power poles.

They checked the condo's generator and said it was wired backwards. They offered to fix it if the condo would open enough rooms to house their people and the rest of FEMA as well. The condo owners agreed and Gibson had it up and running in record time.

There was no security staff anywhere on the island that Jerry could hire. He was able to work with the Chief of Police to find a way to pay for security by hiring off duty police people. Jerry was glad to get them as they were already qualified and experienced. An added advantage was that the locals knew them and respected them. He hired 85 of them. The only police station on the island had a lot of damage as well and FEMA was able to assist them with repairs.

During that typhoon the wind speeds were the fastest ever recorded for a typhoon. It registered at 345 mph. then the tower that registered wind speed blew down. Many of the stores and homes were completely destroyed and most of them had at least some damage. In most cases it was the metal roofs. Since Guam had no natural resources everything had to be shipped in. The houses in Guam were built out of concrete. Guam is one great big rock. The builders dig down to bed rock then build on that so that only the roofs were damaged. Cars and boats were wrecked and all the foliage was stripped away. Everything was brown. Jerry was amazed to see that within only three weeks everything started to grow again. Flowers, bushes, trees all came back. Everything smelled great, clean and new.

The people there were the happiest, friendliest, most open people Jerry has ever known. To them, "life is a beach." They were great family people and even with all that they lost they could smile and laugh. They just didn't take life too seriously. They had a fiesta going every day. The original Spanish name for the island translated to "The Island of Laughing People."

During World War 2, the Japanese took the island and decided to round up the natives, put them in a compound and kill them all. Then a plane flew over the compound and dropped packages of Lucky Strike cigarettes with a note on each pack. It said "Keep faith we are coming soon. The Americans". The Japanese said "Oh shit." so instead of killing them all they put them to work as slave labor building defensive installations. As soon as the Americans landed the natives snuck out to the American lines and told them where all the fortifications were and how to get to them without being seen. You can still see them today.

Jerry found it interesting that after the Japanese treated them so horribly that they now catered to them for their business. They were now the prime tourist location for Japan. During World War 2, war supplies were flown in from the Philippines and green tree snakes came in on the crates. Today they have killed every bird on the island. There are no birds at all, not even sea birds.

Guam has a baseball stadium and Major League teams. They also have a pretty good football team. Several of the team members were working for FEMA and Jerry would often go to their games. While he was there a team from Japan challenged them to play an exhibition game. They agreed and Jerry and other FEMA members went to see the game. The Guam people had a rag tag collection of uniforms from several different clubs, while the Japanese team had all brand new uniforms, shoes, helmets and gear. Jerry was glad to see the Guam team beat the shit out of the Japanese.

Every day Jerry and crew were invited to attend a meal. The folks would almost become offended if they did not come. There was table after table of heated serving trays with all you could eat of all kinds of food and they served beer and liquor as well. With 18 villages there was a fiesta going all the time. Down the beach for a 1/4 of a mile there were Gazeboes all along the shore. You could rent them for your party. They each had a BBQ, water, a sink and power. All you had to do was call ahead and it was yours for the day.

One day Jerry was at one of the picnics and one kid kept sneaking in and stealing BBQ chicken off the grill before things were ready. His mother kept telling him to stop it, but he paid no attention to her. Finally she asked Jerry if he would yell at him for her. Jerry watched and when he sneaked over to grab another piece he boomed out in his loudest, most authoritive voice, "DROP THAT." The boy did, but also a woman at the next Gazebo over dropped a whole tray of food. She came over laughing and told Jerry, "You scared the shit out of me." The boy kept an eye on Jerry all day and didn't steal any more chicken.

Jerry and the police chief became good friends. Jerry got to know his wife who had a hula business. She taught dancing and sold hula supplies. She also put on shows with her dance troupe at the hotels and resorts. She was a beautiful woman who spoke five languages. She could handle the drunk men better than anyone. If they tried to come up on the stage she could get them down with no problems. Her father was actually one of the people who built the fortifications during WW2.

One of the police men had a reputation as the best fisherman on the island. He always caught the biggest fish. He had a 14' boat with a flat bow. He would lay on the bow looking down into the water and move slowly along until he spotted a big fish then he would "free dive" down with his spear and get it. He usually supplied the fish for the fiestas.

The chicken flu came from China and a lot of the people got sick. They did not want to go to the local hospital as their idea of "sterile" was not the same as ours, so they went to the Navy hospital. Jerry had a boil on his leg and had to have it removed at the Presbyterian hospital. The doctor was amazed that Jerry could talk on the phone conducting business while he operated. He had given him a shot for pain and began to operate when Jerry's phone rang. The doctor was dressed in a Hawaiian shirt, flip flops and cut offs. It cost Jerry $144.00.

The Governor of Guam threw a party for the FEMA team at the beach at Anderson AFB. The entire island was surrounded by a reef so Jerry and his crew had to attend a lecture when they first got there about what to do while swimming. They were told to be very careful about the large amounts of water that came over the reef. There were holes in the reef and the current going out would flow down the sides of the reef until it reached one of the holes then shoot out all at once. It could reach 10 to 15 mph. and suck a swimmer right out to sea.

A Puerto Rico man working for FEMA defied all rules. He was loud and boastful but got away with a lot as he was very good looking. He was supposed to stay "low key", drive a non-descript car and not show off. He instead went out and rented a red Ford Mustang convertible. He didn't pay any attention to any of the rules or practices that FEMA recommended.

On the beach at the party there was a big billboard sign there that said "DANGER - DO NOT SWIM IN THIS AREA - DANGEROUS OUT CURRENT" Well, Mr. Puerto Rico did not think it applied to him, so he talked a black woman, and of all people, the safety manager into going swimming with him. They got out about waist deep and started to swim and were immediately swept out to sea past the reef. Jerry asked locals to call the fire department rescue but they said "Oh no, don't bother, the Tigers have got them by now." Jerry grabbed his binoculars and a guy with a note book and said to start a log of everything that happened.

He called the Fire Department, Police and Air Force and requested a helicopter. They didn't have one and called the Navy base. It never showed. The Police launched a rescue boat and the Fire Dept. came with two jet skis on a trailer. All the men came to the trailer and moved the skis to the water by hand. Only one ski ran. The rider was out jumping waves and didn't seem to be looking. Jerry had been watching his people with the binoculars and tried to tell him where they were but he was going in the wrong direction. The Puerto Rico man and the safety man did the right thing and swam to right angles and got out of the current and back toward the reef.

At the safety class they took they were told that the waves acted like a washing machine, banging them into the reef then going straight down and up and back on the reef, over and over. The sharp reef would tear someone up. Jerry was watching and making notes. The safety man got lucky when a big wave picked him up and threw him over the reef, he just got a few scratches. The Puerto Rico man kept trying to climb over the reef and kept getting "recycled". He was getting chewed up but finally a big wave picked him up as well and threw him over the reef.

Jerry kept trying to tell the Fireman where the black woman was but they didn't believe him and wouldn't go the right way. The police showed up and Jerry talked to them and sent them right to her. When they plucked her out of the water there were four Tiger Sharks swimming around her. The smallest was ten feet long. While the sharks watched her and brushed against her, she had not been bitten. They theorized that because she was black and her suit was black and she wore no jewelry, nothing to flash, the sharks weren't sure what she was. Since there were no seals in the area they did not know if she was food or not. They were not used to something that was all black. That probably saved her life. They took her to the hospital to be checked out but she was not hurt, just totally exhausted.

Jerry knew his Field Coordinating Officer, who was (appointed by the President) needed to know about all this, but he had left early. Jerry finished the report log they were keeping and went to the FCOs apartment. He knocked then beat on the door before the FCO answered. He was undressed and was with the female community awareness program officer. Jerry told him to get some clothes on and get to the hospital.

Jerry went back to his office and wrote a detailed report for the FCO. He had the choice of firing the Puerto Rico man or making a hero out of him. The FCO decided to make a hero out of him!

As time went by FEMA helped to rebuild the destroyed wooden houses and a lot of galvanized roofs. They distributed 1,000s of tarps for temporary cover and had ship loads of corrugated roofing material and supplies coming in.

Gibson Electric got the power back on in 65 days then they had a huge party at the pool. Two female FEMA people got involved. Jerry warned them to be careful. At sun down the party moved into town. They got into trouble and one ended up getting fired and the other demoted.

Jerry had to make one decision that really bothered him. One woman who everyone liked and worked several disasters with them, got a DUI before coming to Guam. When she was interviewed she did not tell anyone. When they did the regular background check on her they found out and Jerry had to let her go. He really liked her and did not want to, but had no choice. He said that had she told the truth it would not affected her job at all, but you just can't lie on a government form.

Jerry was in Guam for 97 days. When it came time to check out he had a tingle in his throat. He kept trying to cough it out. By the time he got to Honolulu he was definitely sick. Customs was on one side of the airport and departure on the other. The airline can't handle luggage and you carry your own. While walking across the airport he passed out. They were not going to let him leave on the plane and wanted to take him to the hospital. He showed them is I.D. and said he was on a major mission and had to go. They let him on. When he got to Seattle his ears wouldn't clear and were very painful. Then he flew to Spokane, WA and was sicker than a dog for two weeks.

* * * * * * * * * * * * * *

His next assigned state side disaster was an F5 Tornado in Oklahoma City. An outbreak of tornados tore through the country side from May 2nd thru May 8th 1999. There were 152 tornados with a maximum rated tornado of F5. Winds reached 301 mph on May 3rd. The tornado was over two miles wide! The largest hail was 4.5 inches. The tornados did 1.4 billion in damages. There were 50 fatalities and 895 injuries. It was devastating to see the amount of destruction. People's lives, dreams and hopes turned to rubble. Jerry saw a woman's terry cloth slipper embedded in a Corvette's tire. Cars that looked like big basket balls rolled up and stacked on top of each other. He saw the dead body of a horse that looked un-damaged, on top of a stack of cars that looked as if they had been caught in an eddy. He found out that the horse had come from seven miles away.

Some buildings were untouched and the ones next door were flattened. There was horrible ruin in every direction. It was hard to maintain composure in the wake of all the damage.

Jerry was in charge of security for the FEMA office that was meeting as many needs as it could. There were so many that had lost everything and the FEMA people felt almost hopeless. They could offer food, vouchers for lodging and when someone came to them with a loss claim they would send an inspector out to evaluate the loss so they could give them a small business loan or a grant to rebuild. Needless to say, there were a lot of people receiving help.

Whenever Jerry set up a security team hiring local people he always gave them an introductory speech.

He told them what their responsibilities were, what the FEMA rules were, and what was expected of them. He was a stickler on, being on time. It was usually about a 20 min. speech. When the folks he hired were assembled, he told them to feel free to ask any questions they may have. He barely started speaking when a woman raised her hand. He thought, what the heck could she be asking so soon when I haven't even started. He acknowledged her and she said "Honey, ya know, ya all gonna hafta talk slower, yor in Oklahoma now."

One day he noticed one young man walking around his post with three sets of handcuffs, four magazines of bullets for his gun and every accessory possible on his belt. Jerry asked him "Are you expecting a shoot out here?" He stuck out his chest and said "You can never be too careful." Jerry answered "That's true but I don't want you out here looking for trouble."

Jerry had hired a retired Oklahoma City policeman, Ed, and put him in charge of the other local security guards. He asked him what he knew about this kid. He said "Oh yea, we call him Inspector Gadget." Jerry said "Well, he kinda makes me nervous." "Yea, me too." "Tell you what. Put him out in the parking lot so he won't be contacting so many people."

The next morning at 6:00am Jerry came back to work and saw an unmarked police car, (black, black wall tires, steel rims, a cage in back with an antenna on the roof, in the parking lot parked next to one of the security cars. He thought it was the local police and was glad that they were around to help out and say hello. Jerry drove up to them and the guy in the security car drove off. He pulled alongside the unmarked police car and saw it was Inspector Gadget. Jerry asked, "Where did you get the car?" "It's mine." "Did you buy it at a police auction?" "No." "Who put the cage in it?" "I did." "Do you have lights on it?" "Yea, I have lights in the grill, but they are yellow." "What's the antenna for?" "I have a police scanner," he said proudly. Jerry said "As long as you are working for us, you don't use any of this." "Ok." he answered.

Jerry went into the building and contacted Ed. I want this Inspector Gadget gone by noon and replaced. That kinda guy is trouble waiting to happen. I am not going to be responsible for vicarious liability. At noon Jerry went out and told the kid to go to lunch and not to come back. He was fired. The kid asked him why and he said "You need to drop this dumb charade. You are heading for nothing but trouble from here on. If you want to be a cop, join the academy and be one, don't pretend."

One of the outlying towns had been a main stop for the big cross country cattle drives in days of old. He was in charge of supplying local security to the city hall that was in the bank building. The folks there told him that the Dalton gang had robbed their bank. The town was in good shape but the tornado had almost destroyed the outskirts.

The main FEMA office was in the hospital in Oklahoma City. They were in a section that had once been a children's trauma center. Many of the locals believed it was haunted. Someone was putting tape on the doors, scribbling with a felt marker on the floors, pulling the tape out of the typewriters and they often heard funny noises. Two of the men Jerry hired quit. One was a retired policeman. There were several underground passages going from the hospital to other locations. They were well lighted, ventilated and had linoleum floors. Jerry was never sure what the passages were for but he had to be sure no one was using them without permission. He went in on Sunday mid-day to check on everyone and found a major "Ghost scare" going on. He caught one man running around waving his gun back and forth. This guy had been a problem for some time. When he first tried to enter the building and the guard asked him to show his I.D. he refused and said "I don't have to show my I.D. I am the Major General. The guard called Jerry and when he got there the man said the same thing. Jerry said "I don't give a fuck who you think you are. If you don't show your I.D. you're not getting in." When he caught him running around waving his gun he marched him into his office and reamed his ass. Then Jerry went out into the main office and said "I've had enough of this bull shit about ghosts. I don't want to hear another word about it."

Jerry was there for six months trying to help with the rebuilding of the area. It took a lot of work by a lot of people, but slowly things began to come together.

* * * * * * * * * * * * * *

Jerry's next assignment was covering a flood in Davenport, Iowa. The Mississippi River had caused a lot of damage. When he got there the F.P.O. called him into his office and asked him to read a report he had gotten from a woman in public relations. She stated that "There was massive devastation, dead animals floating in several places, snakes in people's homes and unsanitary conditions everywhere." The F.P.O. had not seen this and asked Jerry and the safety manager to go out and check it out. They spent the day checking the area and interviewed 72 households in the worst part of the flooded area. None had snakes or knew anyone who did and they were not aware of any dead animals in the area. The only dead animal that Jerry saw the whole day was a mouse. There was a lot of flood damage but the water had receded and folks were stating to clean things up, most with FEMA help.

When they got back to the office they wrote up their report and left it up to the F.P.O. to handle it. The woman left shortly after that.

* * * * * * * * * * * * * *

Severe flooding in North Dakota sent many of the FEMA people to Bismarck to help folks in the area. Jerry just got there and had just been introduced to the F.P.O. and a native man, Roger, who was the liaison between FEMA and the tribe. That night Roger went out drinking and really tied one on. He went back to his hotel late, met a woman in the hall way and offered money for sex. She agreed and they went into his room. He was going to pay her but discovered he didn't have enough money left. He realized that he was too drunk to drive so he gave the woman the keys to his FEMA rental car and his government credit card and told her the PIN number and told her to go to the bank and get the money out! This should have ended right here with her leaving with all his money and car, right? She would have disappeared in the night. But no, she goes back with the money and they have sex. He goes to sleep, actually passes out. In the morning, his credit card is there but the car and the woman are gone. He comes to work and tells Jerry that someone stole his car. Jerry calls the police and they come over and Roger tells his story to them. The only difference is that he tells them that he woke up in the morning and his car and keys were gone.

Jerry's desk is just inside the door and while Roger is talking to the police, giving them a description of his car and showing the lease for the rental agreement, Jerry sees a car drive up and park out front that matches Roger's description. A trashy looking woman got out and walked toward the office. "Hey Roger, is that your car out there?" Jerry asks. Roger said "Oh shit and that's her driving it too." Cops start to run out and grab her, but Jerry says, "No wait a minute she's coming in." She comes right to Jerry's desk and says "Hey Roger, you told me to take your car home last night but when I went back to the hotel this morning you weren't there. I didn't know what to do so I brought it here." They put Roger in a separate office and asked her what happened. She was very up front about it and told them everything in full detail. But they found out the "she" was really a "he" and he had AIDS. They brought Roger into the room and told him the facts. He was fired, charged with inappropriate behavior, unlawful use of a government credit card and filling a false police report.

Then, because AIDS is infectious and a potentially fatal illness, they had to notify his wife. He was never seen again.

Once a week Jerry had to drive 650 miles to visit the outer stations helping with the stricken areas. He would leave Bismarck. go to Fargo, Grand Forks, Devil's Lake, Minot then back to Bismarck.

Most of the country was flat and straight with no curves or hills. He decided to make a little time and was doing 115mph when he saw a police car coming after him.

167

He pulled over and when the County Sheriff came up to his car, he showed him his badge and I.D. The Sheriffs said "Why were you going so fast?" "You want the truth?" "Yea." "I was just trying to find a hill or a curve." The Sheriff laughed and said "Don't suppose it would do any good to tell you to slow down?" "No, not really." "OK, well, try to keep it on four wheels."

* * * * * * * * * * * * * *

When Hurricane Georges hit Puerto Rico Jerry was sent to help. It was a category 3 storm that did $2 Billion in damages and killed eight people.

They were in San Juan and he soon learned that all traffic laws were optional and now, with all the street lights and signs down and gone it was everyone for themselves. There was considerable wreckage, with windows blown out, roofs gone, trees down and most vegetation stripped. The first day there Jerry drove a rental car and the F.C.O., safety manager and a real estate agent toured the area to find a building suitable to rent for their office. They looked at fifteen sites.

As they were driving they came upon a police car in the middle of the road with all four doors standing open and no one there. They looked up the street and there was a violent mob coming toward them. They were carrying clubs and some had guns. The hillside road on their left was blocked with traffic and there was a line of cars behind them. There were people everywhere and nowhere to go.

Jerry yelled "HOLD ON!" then cranked the wheel to the left, squealed the tires and went up on the sidewalk and drove down it the whole block then turned onto a clear road and got the hell out of there. They later found that the riot was over ICE! The police officers were badly beaten and two people were killed. They ended up renting the least desirable building, a 1/4 of a block long, 10 stories high, no parking, for more than it was worth as it belonged to the FCOs brother-in-law.

FEMA had barges arriving daily with supplies. They were bringing food, water, medical supplies and ice. FEMA was giving it away but a group of hoods kept trying to steal it so they could sell it. Jerry had to hire armed guards to protect the warehouse on the dock, the barges and the delivery trucks and drivers.

They were starting to fix up the rental and the communications department wanted to get a piece of 3/4" plywood cut in half to mount the switch board. The laborers were arguing about how to cut it. Jerry watched for 20 minutes and finally went out and said "Gimmy the fuckin' saw and get out of the way." Then he cut it.

They were watching one of the trucks being unloaded. Traffic was light and there was a policeman on every corner as the signals were still out. A man came flying up on a "Cafe' Racer" motorcycle with a high R.P.M., drives in front of the building and fires three shots from the bike. The cops did not react in any way. Jerry couldn't believe his eyes, "What the fuck?" A local man said "Hey mon, no problem, he didn't hit any-thing."

There was a whole street of Casinos below Jerry's apartment building. He was on the fifteenth floor and could see a lot of the city. There was a shooting down there every night. Jerry knew it was a tough town when he saw that on every building the first three floors had barred windows and doors.

Jerry was stationed there for seven months. For the Christmas holidays he was able to send for his wife and kids and his apartment was large enough for all of them. Laura was 15 then and Lenny was a year younger. They went to the beach the first day and had their shoes and towels stolen when they went swimming. Laura was accosted by a grown man and they got out of there. From then on they wouldn't go down there without Jerry.

Everyone was told not to wear jewelry and all FEMA employees were told not to wear anything that would identify them as FEMA workers. It seemed the "hoods" assumed that they all had money and would rob and sometimes beat them. Jerry bought the kids belly boards, snorkels, masks and fins. As long as he was with them they had a great time. He rented a car for his wife, but after trying to drive it for just a half day she took it back. Even some of the FEMA people refused to drive. Jerry got to the point where he made up his mind that he would either stay mad at other drivers all the time or get as aggressive as they were. He found out if he pushed harder and showed more balls, that others moved. And, it seemed unbelievable, but no one honked.

He traveled daily to the satellite service centers around the island to be sure that they were getting the supplies they needed to hand out. They gave away food, water, ice and money for hotel rooms to folks who lost their homes. That was one place he was more than happy to leave.

* * * * * * * * * * * * * *

In 1999 Hurricane Lenny hit the U.S. Virgin Islands. Winds reached 155 miles per hour. There were over $ 1.6 million in damages and two people were killed. Later several bodies were found floating in the ocean near shore. There was enough warning so that 309 people were able to seek safety in storm shelters.

FEMA had five days of food stored in the schools.

Afterwards the Governor declared it a disaster area FEMA sent in six medical assistance teams, three support teams and 2 advanced medical teams. Jerry set up an office in St. Croix. There was considerable damage to buildings and many roofs and windows were destroyed. He had just checked into his hotel when the Community Outreach people came to him and said that they had been out talking to people at a development and offering to help when they were shot at.

The next day Jerry and his boss got a car and drove out to the same apartment complex development and they drove in and were shot at. It seems there was a turf war with the local hoods and they didn't want FEMA helping anyone in their territory. Jerry went back to their office and called the local police. He talked to the commander and he said "We don't go in there. We are out gunned if we do." It is a police free zone. Jerry went back to the office and called the FBI, in Washington and told them that Federal employees were being shot at and locals could not or would not do anything. The FBI sent a SWAT team of twenty men. Two nights later they drove into the complex in three vans and got shot at right away. All three vans erupted and the teams bailed out. According to a local, "The FBI kicked the shit of them, made several arrests, confiscated several guns and lots of ammo. They stayed three weeks and as they got info from the hoods they arrested, went out and arrested more. They flushed the whole development in two weeks

*   *   *   *   *   *   *   *   *   *   *   *   *   *

Chapter 7
The 911 Disaster

Jerry was working in Greenville, Tennessee after heavy flooding there. He was supplying security for personnel and helping flood ravaged people. While traveling around to assess the damage he saw his first tobacco field. Farmers were trying to save what they could, hauling it to the dryers. It was interesting that they continued holding car races and football games. During his time off he decided to go to a college game. He sat down on the side with the least amount of people, but did not know anything about either team.

During the game he witnessed the opposite team wearing T shirts with profane sayings and heard chants that were filthy. He couldn't believe it and was disgusted to think that an institute of higher learning would act that way. There were families there with small children and the other fans were shouting nasty dirty things in their faces. Now Jerry is far from a prude, but even he would not talk, let alone shout things like that at a family. He finally was so disgusted that he left the game, went back to his hotel and wrote a letter to the newspaper. He said that he was a traveler that enjoyed going to local sporting events. He could not enjoy the game because of the nasty, dirty calls that a college of highly educated people were shouting at families.

Well, the shit hit the fan. There was an unheard of number of letters written to the paper, including one from the college Dean. He apologized to the people and assured them that steps would be taken to correct the problem and it wouldn't happen again. Some of the other

172

fraternities also wrote apologizes vowing to stop the problem. Several letters were written by folks supporting Jerry's letter and agreeing that it needed to stop. They were especially angry that someone with no ties to either team and was attending as a guest felt appalled enough to write to the paper. Jerry was amazed and pleased that his letter stirred up such a hornet's nest. The newspaper printed an invitation to "the writer", to tour the college to show that they weren't all bad and were taking steps necessary to fix the problem. Jerry did not attend. That was not his goal. He just wanted them to know how bad it looked to an outsider.

Meanwhile FEMA was arranging small business loans and loans to help repair flood damaged homes. They were also providing food, shelter and medical assistance to folks.

After two months there, Jerry and the FCO were trying to show FEMA why it was necessary to keep security in place until the event was over. Jerry was called into the FCOs office when the news program they were watching was interrupted and the plane flying into the tower was shown. The FCO asked Jerry while barely holding back tears, if he thought it was a accident. He said it was highly suspect, he couldn't believe a plane would come in that low. The FCO was on the phone to Washington D.C. when the second plane hit. She turned around to tell Jerry to double the security but he was already doing it. He called the Sheriff and asked if they had a marked patrol unit that wasn't being used that would be available for a while. They had one with a blown engine that they couldn't afford to fix for a couple of months. With their permission Jerry had it towed and parked in front of the DFO. Then he hired an additional guard.

The next day Jerry got a phone call from Washington D.C. office. They wanted him to respond to New York. Jerry said it was impossible because of the message they were trying to send. He couldn't just walk

out days before this disaster ended, it would send the wrong idea.

They agreed and asked him to respond right afterwards. He said he did not want to go as he had been working for the last three months straight and needed to take care of problems at home.

He finished up in Tennessee just as the "no fly" ban was dropped and flew home. His wife was there at the airport to pick him up and told him that FEMA called twenty times and wanted him to call right away from the airport. He called and they begged him to go to New York. They were having trouble with the command staff there and as he had a reputation of being able to deal with difficult people they needed him to help work things out. So, he grudgingly got back on a plane, as they already had his ticket in place, and went to New York. He couldn't believe what he saw. It was terrible. Death and destruction was everywhere.

Police and Firemen where risking their own lives in an attempt to save other. Time and again Jerry saw grown men in tears as they discovered another body. They would often be black with soot from head to toe. Many would collapse from fatigue and from the populated air all around them. In spite of it they pushed their bodies to the limit trying to find even one more survivor in the rubble.

Emotions were running high and many of the responders were torn between despair and anger. They wanted to show their frustration by showing the world that America was ready to fight back. They found ways to display our flag everywhere possible.

When he got there he was told that only a few senior people could rent a car and they had one waiting for him. He picked up his car and went to his hotel. It was 11:00 pm by now and he was dead tired. He lay down for a short nap, but was up in two hours and on the way to the DFO. It was located on a pier. There were already some FEMA people there and a man, who was Jerry's junior, was acting as lead.

Jerry asked how he was getting along with the FPO and he said "Ok." Jerry took a look at the "prospective" and saw that they intended to set up a disaster assistance service center. This was something they had never done before.

This would be a very large center with 14 agencies from city, state and federal working under one roof and coordinated by FEMA. That looked like a real challenge

and Jerry really wanted it.   He told the young man who had taken the lead that he thought he was doing a good job and was very competent.   Then the two of them went in to meet the FCO. Jerry dropped his files on the FCOs desk and said with a smile "You are really screwed now. You're stuck with us. You've already sent three good people home and if you try to send us home it will reflect on you."   The FCO grumbled, but agreed.

Jerry and the young agent went back to his office. He half expected Jerry to take over. Jerry said that everything he could see said that the young man was doing a good job, and he didn't want any part of it. He wanted to set up and run the disaster center.

They had already found a building, but the building manager was being very difficult.   Jerry met with him and talked with him. The manager started telling Jerry what he could and could not do. So, Jerry took him to lunch to get him away from his underlings so he wouldn't need to appear as Mr. Macho, and explained how things were going to be whether he liked it or not. BUT, he also said that they could work together so that they would make most of the modifications to the building appear to be his ideas so he still looked like he was in charge of the building. From then on, he and Jerry got along great. They met once a day and everything worked well.

The entrances had to be changed for security, some doors added and the "flow" of the floor had to be adjusted. Traffic patterns had to keep folks moving from the time they came in until they left out another doorway. Security equipment had to be moved in and the other fourteen agencies needed to be in place. They were serving over 600 people per day.

When Jerry first saw the horrible ruin, all he could think of was that it would take years to clean up. There was so much death and destruction everywhere. He had to be careful to keep as busy as possible to keep his mind off of it. He had a lot to do. He tried to stay focused. He had to hire guards, talk with the various agencies to let them know what they needed to do and coordinate all the things that needed to be done. He needed to bring in supplies and equipment, set up desks and get the staff in place. He needed to make rules regarding who could come and go into the building and how to police it. He supplied flow charts to show how people could get from one agency to another, worked out emergency procedures with police and fire personal and made sure they knew who was where. FEMA had a badge making machine and everyone that worked in the building needed a badge to get in. However Jerry was not comfortable giving FEMA badges to other agencies.

He called Washington, D.C. and talked them into designing a new badge. This one had DASC on it. (Disaster Assistance Service Center). The supervisor of each of the other agencies had to give him a list of the people who worked for them and if their name was not on the list they did not get a badge and were not allowed into the building. If a person was excluded from the building Jerry took his badge and he couldn't get back in. He had to put twenty people out for stealing office equipment from the supply room.

There was a long line of 50+ refrigerator trucks parked outside. They were full of dead bodies. Jerry needed to post armed guards for them as hoods tried to break in to them.

A lot of the people didn't like all the security. It was the same as any airport. They would try to get in without going through it. Some would refuse to go through. So they didn't go in. The wait in line was often six hours. There were signs posted all along the side walk warning that no weapons were allowed and they would be scanned. People would wait the whole time but when they got to where they could see the security equipment they would step out of line and leave. Did they have weapons? Who knew? There were a lot of people trying to scam their way in. They had phony I.D. phony pay slips and one Asian woman came through several times before they caught her. She had thirty-five complete I.D.s in her purse and had already gotten $30,000.00 in cash. There were illegal aliens who got in with phony social security numbers and I.D.s.

New Yorkers learned that if you intimidate the interviewers you can get money from them just to get rid of the problem. Jerry said "No way in hell is this going to work here." He gave each of the interviewers a three foot lath with a bright orange 4" ball on top. "If you feel threatened or frightened of an individual, hold this up and we will be there." This happened about ten times a day. The guards stationed through-out the building all had radios and were told that if there was a ball in the air to call him right away. The guards would not intervene unless there was physical assault. FEMA agents had to handle everything else. They would tell the person to leave and tell them, if you can't get along today maybe you can try again tomorrow. Jerry could tell that the offenders wanted to fight but perhaps not him. He would accompany them out the door.

He worked fourteen to sixteen hours a day and only twice was able to finish a meal without being interrupted.

The building had big windows all the way down the line and each had fans that brought outside air into the building. The particulates in the air were so bad and the window fans did not have any filters on them. Their white inside fans, desks, computers and badge machine and in fact, just about everything else, would be black within a short time. Everything needed to be cleaned four times a day.

Jerry asked for respirator masks on three different occasions and was turned down. He had guards collapsing on the job. The safety department said that there were no toxins in the air. The FCO said they did not want to alarm the public. The EPA was forced to lie about the toxins as they didn't want to close down Wall Street that was just three blocks away. They knowingly sent workers into a hazards situation with no protection and no regards to their personal safety for the countries financial stability.

Jerry went to China Town and bought five masks with his own money and issued them to the outside guards. It was the best he could do. None of the inside workers had them. Even then he was criticized for doing that. He said "Tough shit."

The doors would open at 8:00am but Jerry would be there between 6:30 and 7:00am. The line would already be two blocks long. Anyone who lived within a certain radius and could show proof of loss could qualify. People all over the United States had donated money to help. The Red Cross took in over $300,000,000.00. They had their own security and he came to see Jerry. Jerry said it was nice of him to come by but this was a FEMA operation, so he would not be needed. It was a group policy not an individual agency policy. At first the Red Cross took half of the money and tucked it away into their coffers for further disasters. When the public found out they raised hell. After that the Red Cross made sure to disburse it all.

At one point Jerry asked them if they could go out and distribute water and candy to all the folks having to stand in line for six hours. They agreed and drove their van along handing water and small candy bags to people. The hand outs were free but soon people were breaking into the vans and stealing it. They had to call Jerry to help them get back in one piece.

After eighty-eight days Jerry got sick and left. He thought it was a bad chest cold. When he got home two days later he could hardly breathe and went to his local doctor. The doctor thought he had asthma then found out it was a lot worse and sent him to a lung doctor. That doctor could not figure it out either, he knew Jerry's lungs were deteriorating but didn't know why. He sent his findings to FEMA and they wanted a second opinion so they sent him to another doctor. This man did a much longer series of tests and even called New York to try to get information but came up empty. Jerry was impressed with him as he was very systematic, exploring every avenue available. A much better doctor. He then went back to his doctor who had received the report from the other doctors. This doctor said "Well, you need to get your affairs in order you have less than a year to live!" Jerry said "Fuck you, you son of a bitch, you're fired." He walked out fuming. No one but God could tell him when he would die. When he went home and told his wife she said "I've always been married to a stud and I don't want to live with a cripple." She moved out and got a job in Portland.

Jerry tried to explain her behavior to the kids and as sick as he was, tried to think what he could do. He called the second doctor, Doctor Baylor and tried to get an appointment, but his secretary said that he was not taking any new patients. Jerry then went to his office, and sat there all day, hoping he would come out and talk to him. The secretary kept trying to make him leave and even threatened to call the police. He told her to go ahead that he wasn't leaving until he talked to the doctor. Jerry came back the next day and this time brought his lunch.

About two thirds through the day the doctor came out and talked to him. He did not remember that Jerry was the guy from the 911 disaster so Jerry told Doctor Baylor what happened and that he fired his old doctor and wanted him to take his case. The doctor said "This is really interesting. I would like to find out more about this. I will accept you as a patient. Judy sign this man in as a patient." She was not very happy about it and when he came back for his appointment and started to give his name, she snarled, "I KNOW WHO YOU ARE."

Jerry had three appointments with Doctor Baylor and the doctor was very frustrated as he could get no information from New York. Unknown to Jerry he hopped on a plane to New York and met with the head of research at Mount Sinai medical center. When he came back he told Jerry that he and the research doctor had really hit it off and became friends. He now had a better understanding of what was going on. He started by giving Jerry a battery of tests. MRI, CTs, diaphragm tests, blood tests, blood flow, blood gasses, blood oxygen, and more with long names that Jerry couldn't pronounce.

When all the results were back he called Jerry into his office and said "There was a treatment we gave patients for T.B. in the past that has been modified for your problem. It is still experimental and may or may not work. And there is a possibility it could kill you." Jerry answered "What have I got to lose I am dying anyway?"

The doctor set it up for Jerry and he went into the hospital. He would have the bottom part of his lungs, that were dissolving, scared to stop the progression. It was an overnight procedure. They wanted him to stay in the hospital for three days but he knew the kids needed him and talked the doctor into letting him go the next day. There was no one to pick him up so he drove himself. He was so sick he barely made it home. He was trying to get things in order as he planned to move to Portland in hopes of saving his marriage. He was alone in the house when he got dizzy and collapsed in the dining room. All he could think was that he didn't want the kids to come home and find him lying on the floor dead.

He tried to crawl to the bedroom and it seemed as though it was taking forever. He finally got there and managed to pull himself up on the bed. He heard a voice coming from the dining room. It sent a chill down his back as it was the very distinct voice of a very close friend who had passed away two months earlier. "Hey Jerry," said the way he always said it every time they met. Jerry said "What do you want Tim?" he answered, "Common it's time to go." "I can't go Tim, I've go two kids to take care of and they need me." "I can't come back." he responded, Jerry said "Why not?" He didn't hear another word. Jerry went to sleep on the bed thinking he would never wake up, but he did.

The kids had both graduated from high school and Lenny had moved out. Laura was about to. They both spent a lot of time with their Dad though and talked about moving to Portland. Jerry was able to sell the house quickly and started packing things up.

Something strange began to happen. From the time they had moved in to that house both kids had made comments about hearing funny noises. Nothing really scary, just odd. Every time they needed to go into the basement for some reason they would insist on taking their dog with them. One evening Laura had come back down stairs and asked Jerry who the nice old man was that had looked in to her room. She said she was in bed and happened to look up and he was standing at the door looking in and smiled at her then headed down stairs. Jerry told her she probably fell asleep and dreamed it, but she swore there was someone there.

182

Now, as he was trying to get everything into boxes ready to move, things started happening. First he heard a door shut upstairs. He thought one of the kids had come home and gone upstairs, but no one was there. While he was upstairs he heard noises downstairs. Again, no one was there. This happened three more times in the next few hours. He was loading some things into the car and came back in and set his car keys on the dining room table. He went into the kitchen to get another box, set it on the dining room table and his keys were gone! He thought he must have dropped them but they were nowhere in sight. Then he heard another door close upstairs. Now he was getting mad. This was ridiculous. "OK," he hollered "Come down here right now. I have had it with you. We need to talk." He felt stupid but didn't know what else to do. A few minutes went by then he felt a chill in the air. "Now look," he said to the thin air, "We are moving, whether you like it or not. I know you have enjoyed my family being here, but then you also know that we need to move and try to get the family together again. The house has been sold to a nice family and I am sure you will like them as well. So, please leave me alone so I can get done. I am sick enough without you giving me a bad time!" He then went back into the kitchen and got another box and set it next to the first one on the table. His keys were back right where he left them. Nothing else happened. He felt a little guilty with that lie, as in reality the house was sold to a bachelor.

After three weeks Doctor Baylor felt the operation was going to be a success. That led to the use of the treatment on other suffers. It seemed a huge number of first responders were having the same problem and some were dying.

One of the tests Doctor Baylor had Jerry take was sleep study to see if he may have "sleep apnea." He did stop breathing several times during the test as well as exhibiting "restless leg syndrome." Jerry was also diabetic. The doctor set him up with a breathing machine to use during the night and had him carry a portable oxygen machine for day time use. He recommended continuous oxygen.

Jerry's wife had never done any of the household chores. Jerry did all the cooking and laundry and Laura did all the cleaning. His wife had several hobbies and her craft supplies were strung all over the house. Two rooms were so full you couldn't even walk into them. Jerry told her she would have to come back and pack them up herself.

Meantime Jerry had rented an apartment for her in Vancouver and was paying the rent on it. When everything was packed he hired four of Lenny's buddies and they packed two of the largest U Hauls, Jerry's truck and his trailer and moved it all to a storage locker in Vancouver, WA. They then put Jerry's personal bedroom furniture and belongings into the second bedroom of the apartment. His wife wanted her own room. Jerry went back to Wallace and stayed in an R.V. until the house closed. It was supposed to be two days but turned out to be twelve days.

When he got back to Vancouver, the Med Care oxygen supplier met him at the apartment. However there was no place to put the machine as the apartment was crammed full of arts and crafts supplies. There wasn't even a flat place to put the paper work down to sign it. He was so angry and so tired he just said "I give up, fuck this shit, I can't live like this, you knew I was coming. I will pack up in the morning and leave. This is a good place to call a halt to it." Then he threw all the craft supplies that were stacked in his room out in the hall. She just glared at him and he went to bed.

She stayed up all night moving stuff to a storage locker. When he got up the house was clean and neat and all the boxes of craft supplies were gone. He stayed, hoping they could work things out.

They started looking at new homes and found one being built that they really liked. His wife promised that she would do half the house work if he bought it. It was a large home on a corner lot in a very desirable neighborhood in Richfield. They were there eleven and a half months and she only vacuumed once and did dishes once. He finally filed for divorce. He served her with the papers, told her that they needed to sell the house and split the assets. She trashed everything in her room and there was broken glass all over when she left. He put a For Sale by Owner sign in the yard and within a few hours the place sold, papers signed and a earnest money paid. Knowing he was going to file for divorce Jerry had sold his new pickup truck, a Ford F250 diesel with lots of extras and bought an old Ford F100 6cy. Then went to Idaho and he and Lenny purchased a house in Sprit Lake, together. He used the money he got when he sold his truck for the down payment and put the house in Lenny's name. When the Richfield house sold he rented a U Haul and put all his things in the Spirit Lake house.

Although he liked the area and the hunting was good there he still longed for his dream of living in a boat and enjoying the sea.

*   *   *   *   *   *   *   *   *   *   *   *   *   *

Chapter 8

Back to the Sea

After moving his things to the Spirit Lake house he turned around and went back to the coast and bought a 36' Albin Tri cabin Trawler. He stayed on it for four months then put it in dry storage in September and went back to Idaho. Jerry had owned boats most of his life.

During the winter he thought a lot about his dream of living on a boat full time and decided he would pursue that dream the following spring.

Lenny graduated from college and Laura was married and had two fine sons by now. Jerry decided they could spare him a few months at a time and vowed to go after his dream of living on a boat.

He thought that the Albin was a little small to actually live on so he looked for a larger boat. He finally found one and was able to trade the Albin for the down payment on the larger boat. This was a West Port, 52' Yacht with two 375 hp diesel engines. It was in good shape but needed some T.L.C. It was Jerry's dream boat.

He took his 36' Albin to Ludlow and parked next to the new boat and moved all his things over to it. Then he got to work fixing it up the way he wanted it.

He installed new carpet, big T.V., new cook stove, stereo system, new furniture, tinted windows, new electronics, two new GPS with depth sounders, new VHF radios, six new antennas, new Tempurpedic mattress on his bed, and had the heater rebuilt by a professional company (3 times.)

He got a new outboard for the dingy, new down rigers, new fishing rod holders and nets and had the engines gone over completely by a mechanic. He washed it, cleaned everything else added a new ceiling and all other basic maintenance. Next he moved everything on to the new boat. He named her the Spirit Quest.

He bought it in January and finally finished with all the work he wanted done on it the first part of May. He made arrangements with the bank to take automatic payments out of his account so that if he was gone at the time they were due he wouldn't have to worry about them.

Over the next few months he took some of his buddies out for a Salmon derby, then took his ex wife and daughter and her two little boys for a cruise. Jerry had his two sisters, Barbara and Jean along at another time and had a great time. He was thankful to have such great relations with his family. He could be a real pest sometimes pulling pranks on them though.

He spent a few weeks cruising around the San Juan Islands just taking it easy, getting a great tan and fishing. He was living his dream. Then one day while fishing near Port Angles he decided to go to La Push. He was in the straits of Juan de Fuca and was on the fly bridge lashing things down so they would not roll around when he got out into the ocean. He heard a noise, a sound, a buzzing so he looked around and it was coming from the pilot house.

He had a big alarm panel there but couldn't see which one it was. He was heading down below to see which alarm was going off and the second he took his first steep down the ladder a big ball of flame came shooting up toward him.

He spun around and headed right back up with the flames shooting up the stair well right behind him. It burned his hair and melted his shirt, and was coming up his pant leg. Flames blew out the sky light and spread along the side of the boat and were melting the dingy. There was a terrible roaring and smoke was bellowing out of the cabin.

He couldn't get to his radio to call for help or to the sky crane that lowered the dingy and he couldn't lower by hand. He was able to grab a life jacket and was trying to figure out how to get past the flames to get to the dingy. The next thing he knew his oxygen tanks were exploding and shot him into the water.

As he was treading water the boat was floating away and completely engulfed in flames. He was devastated, he had lost everything! It was everything he owned. As he watched he life's dream burn before his eyes he thought about taking the life jacket off and just letting go. What was the use?

The only thing that kept him hanging on was the thought that his children would never find his body and never have any closure. The water was very cold, he had been treading water for over thirty minutes, he felt numb all over, then he started to calm down, began to feel warmer. This he knew was a sign of hypothermia, he just knew he was dead.

Then to his surprise two fishermen in a eighteen foot boat came around his boat and summing up all his energy he waved and shouted. At first no sound came out he had inhaled so much smoke, he could hardly make a sound, but he tried again and was able to get their attention. They were searching around the boat, which was some distance away by now and by chance had glanced his way and finally seen him. He did not think they would be able to get him out, but they plucked him out of the water like a fish.

Meanwhile a larger whale watching boat who had seen the flames and rushed to get there came around his boat and the fishermen took him to that boat. They called the coast guard to tell them there was a survivor and called for a helicopter to rush him to the hospital. He was lifted in a "basket" they lowered and flown to the

hospital. He never did find out who the two men that saved him were but sent them a prayer of thanks.

Jerry was flown to a hospital in Port Angles where he was treated and later released. His yacht was still burning when it sank. Jerry sighed "How do you recoup what you worked your whole life for?"

They told him the black plume of smoke could be seen thirty miles away. He learned later that some forty or so people on the shore and in other boats had called into report the fire. It was the talk of the whole area in 2006.

Three news crews had picked up the story and videos of his boat burning where on two news channels. The next day a person from the Good Morning America T.V. show contacted him and asked if they could interview him for a segment on the show. He agreed and they came in with their cameras and lights and the story was aired with Dana Salyer interviewing him.

When Jerry was to be released from the hospital he had to call his son Perry who lived in Seattle as he had no clothes and no transportation. Perry and his wife Anglia knew what had happened, had in fact seen it on the news and immediately gone out and bought a jogging outfit, shoes and underwear for him. Perry met him at the hospital and took the clothes to him then drove Jerry to his sister Jean's house in Sedro Woolly where Jerry had left his car. They picked up a new cell phone, then went back to Perry's home and Perry asked Jerry to stay with them for a while. It seems that Perry and his son were supposed to go out on the boat that day with Jerry, but Perry got called in to work and couldn't go. Jerry was thankful that the two of them were not there. His grandson could have died from the cold water and perhaps his son as well.

It took Jerry a couple of months to get the insurance company to settle his claim. He had insurance and they were not going to pay as they claimed that since the boat sunk, they could not tell if it was an accident or Jerry did it on purpose. He had to hire a marine attorney who told him that they always do that, but would settle the day before it went to court. That is exactly what they did do.

After he received the settlement he went to Portland and bought a 28 foot Bayliner, and paid to have it hauled to La Push. He spent the rest of the summer on this boat.

In the fall he went back to Idaho and bought a manufactured home in a senior community in Hayden. For the next few years he spent his summers living and fishing on his boat and spent his winters in Idaho. He bought a motorcycle as well and got together with a good friend Pete that he had known since high school. The two of them went on "Man trips." each summer and had a great time.

Both Laura and Lenny lived in the area and he spent a lot of time with them as well. Several times Laura tried to get her Dad to start dating again, but he just wasn't interested. He was doing a lot of cross country riding with his buddy and enjoying his boat and did not feel the need to find another woman. He had already had enough problems with women to last him a life time.

* * * * * * * * * * * * * *

Chapter 9

A Silver Lining Somewhere

Jerry had been a bachelor for seven years now. One day Laura conned him into trying an online dating service. By now Jerry was sixty-five. He was riding his motorcycle, fishing, hunting and basically pretty active despite the fact that he was on oxygen. Laura helped him write a profile and submitted it. He posted a photo of himself standing in front of his motorcycle. He got several emails right away. However most were from women a LOT younger than he. He wrote back to a couple of them asking what they saw in a man thirty five to forty years older than they were. Two wrote back "I don't think a man matures until he is in his sixties." Jerry wrote back, "What you mean is you don't think his wallet matures until he is in his sixties." One lady he met for lunch at a cafe' was so boring he could hardly wait to leave. He was about ready to give up.

One day, after he had been on the site for a few days he got an email from a widow woman who had her own motorcycle, who loved to fish, had her own boat and enjoyed hunting, was his age and lived only a few miles away. They emailed each other then spoke on the phone. He thought she would never stop talking. Then he asked her to dinner, planning on an evening a week or so away.

It just so happened that she was going to be coming his way that very evening as she was a member of The Patriot Guard, a motorcycle club that supported military people It seemed there was a flight of service people coming home from overseas that night and the club was going to welcome them. Each member would hold an American flag and form a double line of welcome for the returning troops as they came down the ramp from the plane. They would cheer and clap for them. She asked Jerry if he would like to go as well. He said he would and offered to buy dinner before the plane arrived. They liked each other right away.

Over the next few months they got to know each other well and found they had more and more in common. Dale loved to fish and had spent her entire childhood fishing with her Dad who was one of those fishermen who caught fish when no one else was even getting a bite, all around him. She also had a boat and lived by the water. She liked to shoot and liked to go hunting although she did not like to actually shoot the animal. No problem with gutting, cleaning and hauling but not the kill.

She also was very impressed with Jerry and everything he had done. She really admired and respected him. Jerry felt comfortable with her and enjoyed the fact that she had her own bike and they could ride together. He was never fond of carrying a passenger on his bike.

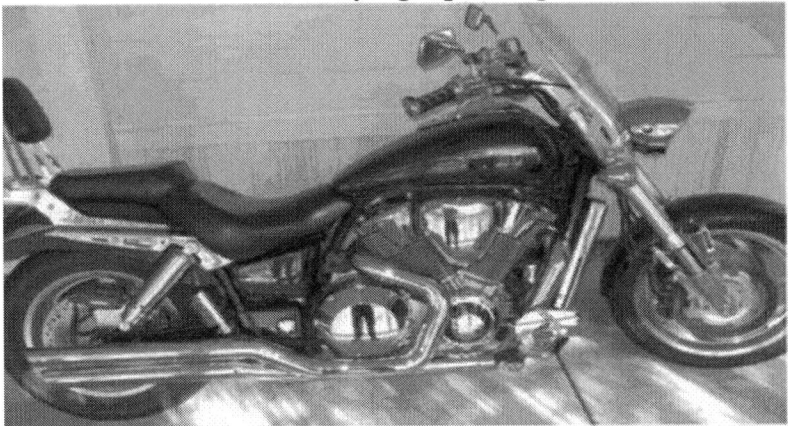

She belonged to three different motorcycle clubs and Jerry met some great people at the different meetings. The clubs were also involved in charity events and rides that he enjoyed. They spent a lot of time on the bikes and went on some great rides. While his bike was a great bike for short rides it was not very comfortable on long trips .

Dale had a Goldwing and Jerry decided that he would get one as well. He knew that it was the "Cadillac," of motorcycles and a lot more comfortable on long trips. So, he decided to look for a Goldwing of his own. Meanwhile he joined the Goldwing clubs that Dale belonged to and looked around for a good deal on a "Wing."

Jerry and Dale had a great time, riding, fishing and hunting. Things were starting to look up for both of them. Jerry finally found a good deal on a Wing and went to west Spokane to see it. As it turned out, the deal was not quite what he wanted but there was room to "dicker." Then someone told him there was one on special at the dealer to the far east Spokane so they went there to check it out. He got a great deal on it and took it home.

Now he was ready for some serious long distance riding. They went on several cross country rides and put about 50,000 miles on the bikes. Over the next few years,

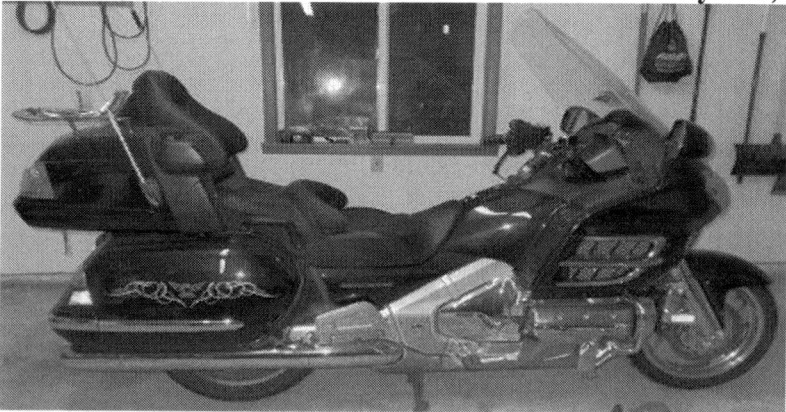

they traveled to almost every state in America, drove through just about every type of weather imaginable, met some great folks, got into some wild situations and adventures and enjoyed life.

As they toured most of the United States they visited most of the National Parks on the bikes. Each year they attended a nationwide motorcycle event and enjoyed the games and companionship of other riders

The clubs had competitions to see which club had the best camp site and dressed for the theme for that year. It was great fun. These were all good people and most events were family oriented.

The Patriot Guard that honored our troops, also provided honor guards at funerals for the members that lost their lives, but only if the family requests it. Jerry and Dale both felt honored to participate but with Jerry's oxygen needs it became too hard for him to stand for the length of time required. They still try to support that group in other ways.

Jerry and Dale go on salmon fishing trips to the coast and enjoy the fishing on their local lake. Now, three years later they are still exploring the world together and working on their bucket list.

As time went on Jerry's lungs got a little worse and his family talked him in to selling his bike. He had to admit that he had a lot of really good years of riding behind him and that his health might slow him down a little. He took their advice and sold his bike but then he and Dale went out and bought a Corvette. No sense slowing down after all. They could still travel all they liked and would be a little safer.

The next summer they took a Corvette tour of all the National Parks in the western half of the United States. Then they went to Las Vegas and spent some time seeing the shows and Dale played the slots while Jerry enjoyed the poker games. Both came away with more than they started with. They had been traveling with the top down on the "vet", but it was so hot in Vegas, they had to put the top back on and turn on the air conditioning.

Jerry later went with his high school buddy Pete to a International Sports Car Rally in Austin, Texas. They got to drive the car around the race track, met the pro race car drivers, and the Corvette girls. Jerry won the plaque for driving his car the longest distance. It was signed by all the professional Corvette race car drivers.

Then they were treated to a great dinner and special treatment in the Corvette Corral room.

On the way home they were able to open the car up on some of the remote highways. In one state they were flying along and a state trooper stopped them. Jerry pulled over and when the trooper asked for his driver's license he opened his wallet and of course his Sergeant Police badge was there as well.

Jerry said "You know, I don't really see what the problem is here. I have a car that is built for speed, a flat open road with no traffic a beautiful day, and I am a trained professional driver." The trooper agreed and said "Well I would worry about your tires." Jerry answered, "These are 200 mile an hour tires." The officer said "OK, but be careful." Then Jerry got an idea. He said "How about doing me a favor? Call ahead and tell the other officers I am coming and that I am a good guy." The trooper said "Sure, I can do that, but I am not sure they will all go for it. We have some young new guys out there. How are they going to know who you are?" Jerry said "Come on now, how many old retired police Sergeant are driving by here at this speed in a

196

metallic red Corvette?" So, the trooper made the call and Jerry was off and running. They were doing over 100 miles per hour and passed several officers over the next 150 miles. As they were leaving the state they saw one more trooper. He was pointing a radar gun at them as they zoomed by, and he stuck his hat out the window and waved to them.

Jerry and Dale have thousands of miles on the Corvette now and are having a ball. They have been visiting family, attending family reunions and special events on the coast, attending Corvette club events and just going for drives around the country.

So, I guess we will close here, as they drive off into the sunset and live happily ever after!

The End

Authors note* More first responders have died from lung problems, than the people who were killed in the original attack.

Notes

Notes

Notes

56885690R00111

Made in the USA
Columbia, SC
02 May 2019